Classic Asian Philosophy

CLASSIC ASIAN PHILOSOPHY

A Guide to the Essential Texts

Joel J. Kupperman

OXFORD
UNIVERSITY PRESS

2001

OXFORD
UNIVERSITY PRESS

Oxford   New York

Athens   Auckland   Bangkok   Bogotá   Buenos Aires   Calcutta
Cape Town   Chennai   Dar es Salaam   Delhi   Florence   Hong Kong   Istanbul
Karachi   Kuala Lumpur   Madrid   Melbourne   Mexico City   Mumbai
Nairobi   Paris   São Paulo   Shanghai   Singapore   Taipei   Tokyo   Toronto   Warsaw

and associated companies in
Berlin   Ibadan

Copyright © 2001 by Joel J. Kupperman

Published by Oxford University Press, Inc.
198 Madison Avenue, New York, New York 10016

Oxford is a registered trademark of Oxford University Press

Library of Congress Cataloging-in-Publication Data
Kupperman, Joel.
Classic Asian philosophy : a guide to the essential texts / by Joel J. Kupperman.
p. cm.
Includes bibliographical references and index.
ISBN 0-19-513334-X—ISBN 0-19-513335-8 (pbk.)
1. Philosophy, Asian. 2. Asia—Religion. I. Title.
B121.K85   2000
181—dc21   00-020488

1 3 5 7 9 8 6 4 2

Printed in the United States of America
on acid-free paper

PREFACE

This book grows out of a perceived need. There has been increased interest in Asian philosophy. One manifestation is the profusion of translations of Asian texts, as well as of books that explore themes connected with those of Asian philosophy. The latter, however, do not include anything that amounts to a clear and straightforward account keyed to what the most widely known Asian classics are about. The intelligent nonspecialist reader who wanders into this area will need a better guide than anything currently available. Also in need of a guide are teachers of philosophy and their students, who can use orientation if they are to explore any Asian philosophical work in much the same spirit as they explore classic texts of Western philosophy.

The need is intensified by the difficulties that many classic Asian texts present to readers coming from the outside. Initially one might suppose that the questions being asked are much the same as those familiar in Western thought, although there may be different answers. Often this turns out not to be the case. The reader then must struggle to get a sense of what is at issue, before beginning to understand what a work has to offer. Some Asian texts also have special difficulties. The great Daoist classic the Zhuangzi, for example, maintains a playfulness and humor that can leave the first-time reader wondering what, if anything, is to be taken seriously. (The answer "everything and nothing," while true, is not helpful.) Confucius presents extraordinary difficulties because of the mosaic-like character of what survives of his thought. Brief sayings, often highly allusive, will seem at first to be extraordinarily cryptic. The reader needs to gain a sense of recurrent themes, along the lines of which one can reassemble the mosaic until patterns emerge. Virtually any reader will need help with this process.

I came therefore to view this book, which is a generalist rather than a specialist project, as an extension of teaching. The organizing principle is simple. Each of the eight chapters focuses on one classic Asian text (or, in one case, cluster of texts), which is widely available in paperback, frequently in more than one translation. Each of these eight books, incidentally, is one that at some time or other I have used as one of the assigned books in an undergraduate course. The goal of each chapter is not only to explicate the text (or texts) but also to make it come alive. That is, we should be able to see Asian philosophers as struggling with important questions, ones that could matter to us too, and as offering answers that (even were we to find in the end that we cannot entirely accept them) would be plausible—in relation to those questions—to an intelligent person.

There is a bonus in coming to understand, and to feel at home in, these texts. This is that they are all to some degree foundational to a culture or cultures. India (represented by three texts) and China (represented by four, plus most of the cluster of Zen texts discussed in the penultimate chapter) are philosophically rooted cultures. By this I mean that philosophies have much the same kind of radiating influence over the thought and categories of these cultures that Homer is sometimes assigned in ancient Greece, Dante in Italy, Goethe in Germany, and Shakespeare in England. To begin to understand the Upanishads and the Bhagavad Gita is to go a considerable distance in understanding India. A similar comment applies to Confucius and the great Daoist texts in relation to China. A case can be made for saying that these Chinese texts also are to a degree foundational to Japanese culture. The influence of China in the early periods of Japanese culture is often not realized. Indeed, the striking fact that most of the best early Japanese literature (including some great poetry and one of the two or three greatest novels ever written, *The Tale of Genji*) was written by women is sometimes explained by the fact that so many of their Japanese male counterparts were writing in Chinese.

There is every reason for providing straightforward accounts of these classic texts and of the problems that generate them. It is only fair to add, though, that the process of arriving at the accounts—whatever the result—cannot be entirely straightforward. Some balancing acts are required. First of all, there is the balancing of specialized knowledge with the general interest of the likely reader. My strategy throughout will be to bring in specialized background knowledge only when it seems very important, and then to introduce it in a way that minimizes disruption of the flow of exposition. Each chapter will conclude with a brief section on recommended reading that includes references to some specialist literature.

A more complicated balancing act is this. The temptation, in trying to come to terms with any Asian texts, is to look for Western parallels. One can say, for example, that some lines of inquiry in the great Confucian philosopher Mencius are very like some in the eighteenth-century Scottish philosopher David Hume; many readers, seeing this, will begin to relax. The technique of looking for Western parallels will work much better in some cases than in others. Even in the best cases, though, it can cause us to overlook something unique and interesting in an Asian philosophy. Often the result will be much worse than this: the Asian philosophy fitted to a Western template will emerge as a crude caricature. My strategy throughout this book will be to balance the use of Western parallels, where appropriate, with probes of what is distinctive and, as it were, untranslatable in Asian texts. Often this approach will amount to a limited use of Western parallels accompanied by warning labels and cautionary remarks.

This project is very much keyed to its time, a moment at which Asian philosophies are coming to seem important but many interested readers have trouble getting the hang of them. It will succeed if many readers come to find Asian philosophical classics much more accessible, and if some of them are enabled to read further and to go beyond what this book is intended to offer.

ACKNOWLEDGMENTS

It is appropriate that this book has benefitted from a variety of networks. The project was reviewed by anonymous specialists in Asian philosophy, both at the prospectus stage and when the manuscript had been completed. I am grateful for these comments, which on the whole were probably kinder than I deserved, and which have saved me from some mistakes. One reviewer whose comments were very helpful, Arindam Chakrabarti, no longer remains anonymous. As first written, the Chinese philosophy chapters were inconsistent in the use sometimes of the new pinyin system of romanizing Chinese names and terms and sometimes of the older Wade-Giles. (Part of the problem is that most of the good available translations, including the two best of the Zhuangzi and the two best of Mencius, predate the introduction of pinyin.) I have followed a reviewer's suggestion in the final version of this book by consistently using pinyin. At first use of a Chinese name or term the Wade-Giles romanization is also supplied in parentheses.

This book is the result of a long process of learning and exploration. It would be impossible to list all of the people whose comments and conversation, at various stages of involvement, have enriched my view. Many of these conversations were with Karen Ordahl Kupperman. Both she and Diana Meyers made helpful comments on a preliminary version of chapter 6. Michael Kupperman was helpful in selecting and formatting an image for the cover. I am endebted to Jerome Smith and Ben Sachs for introducing me to the limitations of raccoon nature (chapter 9). Conversations with Bonnie Smith about the cultural matrix of Asian philosophy also were very helpful. A number of philosophers over the years have talked with me about the connections between Asian and Western philosophy: let me single out Henry Rosemont, Jr., Kwong-loi Shun, and Bryan Van Norden.

My good luck included having (again) an excellent production editor, Robert Milks, and an excellent copy editor, Daphne O'Brien. Any author can appreciate what the benefit is of judicious, helpful, and non-intrusive treatment of a manuscript. Finally, I would like to thank the philosophy editor at the New York Oxford University Press, Peter Ohlin, who suggested that I write this book and whose advice as the project progressed was consistently good.

CONTENTS

Classic Asian Philosophy

ONE

THE UPANISHADS

Most of us at some point in our lives stop to ask who we are. Perhaps we have been playing a part or simply doing what other people expect of us. It does not feel right, and it occurs to us that things would be different if we were our real self. Our real self, we think: what is that?

The Upanishads, written in India mainly in the eighth to sixth centuries BCE, keep asking such questions. The answers are radical. If we accepted them, they would change our lives, probably to the point at which our friends wouldn't recognize us.

Besides having this life-changing potential, the Upanishads also are highly serious philosophy. They develop a sophisticated and (on the whole) highly consistent world picture, a metaphysics that in some respects parallels that developed much later by Baruch Spinoza in the West. As in Spinoza's case, the metaphysics generates an ethics. What the world really is like tells you what the best way is to live.

These early texts also built on preexisting trends within Indian culture. Then their influence had a major role for more than two thousand years in shaping that culture. Thus they are metaphysics, ethics, and basic cultural documents.

In what follows we can approach the Upanishads by stages. First we can look at them informally in relation to the common human problems of life and death, exploring their cultural roots and resonances. Then we can, at much greater length, examine them as a philosophical system.

Life and Death

A disarming introduction to the complex philosophy is provided by a fable in the Katha Upanishad. Nachiketas's father has offered a sacrifice to the gods. Ancient India, like ancient Greece and many other cultures, worshiped many gods and goddesses; and it was considered meritorious to offer them animal sacrifices. What good the sacrifices did the gods was a matter of conjecture, but certainly they were signs of respect or devotion. Nachiketas's father, though, offered his sacrifice out of selfish motives, and not in a spirit of unselfish devotion. This disgusts Nachiketas, and he suggests that his father might as well sacrifice him also. His father, angry, offers him to Death.

As the fable proceeds, Death is not at home when Nachiketas arrives. This lapse of hospitality creates obligations. Death offers Nachiketas three boons. The first two are straightforward: Nachiketas would like to be back on good terms with his father and to understand the sacrifice by fire. The third is more complex. Nachiketas asks about the law of life and death, especially what happens after death.

Clearly this inquiry enters the territory of religion, and the long discussion that follows stamps this as a religious text. Indeed the Upanishads were—and remain—the core texts of Hinduism, which continues to be by far the dominant religion of India and to have adherents in some other countries of South Asia as well.

The Upanishads also are philosophy. Indeed, they are widely viewed as the foundational texts of some major traditions of Indian philosophy, as well as central to the Hindu religion. Further, they are exceptionally subtle and interesting as philosophy.

When is religion also philosophy? No one would want to suggest that the correctness (or lack of correctness) of a religion is a factor. What does matter is the presence of arguments, which may be explicit or implicit, so that what is offered is not merely an appeal to faith or devotion (or to reliance on the authority of the religious text) but instead an argued set of views that then is open to counterargument. It also matters if a text presents a complex and coherent picture of the world in which various elements mutually support one another.

By these criteria the Bible would be generally considered, even by its most fervent admirers, to be a religious text and not a work of philosophy. The fundamental appeal is to revelation and not to a structure of argument. The work of St. Thomas Aquinas (and for that matter John Calvin), on the other hand, although it shares with the Bible claims about God, life, and death, would generally be considered to be philosophy.

What the Upanishads have in the way of argument, and in a structure of mutually supporting views, should be clear shortly. For the time being I ask the reader to open her or his mind to the possibility that what we are considering is philosophy as well as religion.

As religion, the text does not have a message that is easy to understand. The Christian answer (at least in the basic version that had developed by the Middle Ages) to the questions of life and death has tended to be straightforward. The four possibilities after death are heaven, hell, limbo (a place in the suburbs of hell for virtuous pagans, not unpleasant but lacking in the goods of heaven), and purgatory. Virtue, repentance, and faith all figure in accounts of what makes someone eligible for heaven.

Within this basic picture there has been considerable room for movement. Gottfried Leibniz, for example, three hundred years ago defended the view that this is the best of all possible worlds by contending that, even though most people go to hell, the goodness per person of those who go to heaven is greater than the evil per person of those who go to hell (so that the total of goodness is greater than the total of evil). It may be that most religious people today would make a higher estimate of the number of those who are saved.

The ancient Hindu answer to the questions of life and death is tempered by the doctrine of reincarnation, which (again) was shared with ancient Greece. After death one will enter a new life. The ancient Greeks spoke of the river Lethe (forgetfulness) from which one must drink before entering the new life, and the ancient inhabitants of India also tended to assume that in the new life one would remember very little or nothing of the old one. There was the possibility of reincarnation as an animal. The Law of Karma held that how favorable a reincarnation was (i.e., whether it was in a privileged social caste or in a low caste or as an animal) depended in a fairly automatic way on the degree of virtue contained in the old life. It was as if light souls rose and heavy souls sank.

What Death tells Nachiketas is consistent with this picture. But it offers another possibility, one that escapes the endless round of reincarnation (which might seem a tedious prospect). The Upanishads promise that, in a spiritual state referred to as *moksha* (liberation or release), you can have permanent spiritual fulfillment after death. In order to have this, you must follow the path of joy rather than the path of pleasure.

It may be that one of the marks of philosophy, above and beyond the two already mentioned, is that the reader has to think hard about what the words mean. Ordinary words like "knowledge," "causation," and "goodness" take on resonances in philosophical writing that provoke this reflection. "Pleasure" and "joy" certainly are familiar words. But it may not be immediately easy to say what the difference between them is, or whether there is any difference in how you would go about getting pleasure or getting joy. Yet the Upanishads tell you that the nature of your eternal life, and your escape from the cycle of reincarnation, depends on your observing the difference.

Philosophers sometimes are themselves in denial about the provoking opacity of words on which they rely. Some, notably in the utilitarian tradition, have wanted to lump together the whole range of positive emotional states—including pleasure, happiness, joy, euphoria, ecstasy, and bliss—within a general category of gratification, thus ignoring their differences (which are differences in kind, and not merely of degree). But much of Indian philosophy, and some philosophy in the West as well, insists that the differences are of vital importance.

We therefore will have to look closely at pleasure and at joy. First, though, we need to understand the metaphysics of the Upanishads, the picture of the world that underlies the ethical advice about how to prepare for life after death. The metaphysics centers on a single, deceptively simple claim: *atman* is Brahman.

"*Atman* is Brahman"

Atman (pronounced "Aht-man") and Brahman are central to classical Hindu philosophy. Are they central to experience? Perhaps this is not true, at least explicitly, for most of us. But the ancient Indian argument is that it should become true. The right kind of experience is claimed to provide evidence for the identification of *atman* with Brahman.

Let us begin with Brahman. It already has been noted that the ancient religion of India worshiped many gods and goddesses. Three gods were paramount: Brahma the creator, Vishnu the preserver, and Shiva the destroyer. If it seems strange that a god of destruction is one of the three main gods, reflect on what it would be like in the world if nothing ever was destroyed or died. The world would become undesirably cluttered, and also stagnant. There also are major goddesses, the most important being the great goddess Devi (whose transmutations in Indian tradition were wonderfully illustrated by a great Devi exhibit in Washington in 1999).

One needs to be mindful of the difference between Brahma, who is merely one god, and Brahman, who is everything. With the idea of Brahman, Hinduism makes the transition to a religion of a single divine reality. This transition was accomplished in different ways by different cultures. The simplest way is to deny that the gods and goddesses your ancestors worshiped really exist. Zoroaster in ancient Persia came up with an ingenious twist. The many gods, *devas*, who had been worshiped did exist, but were evil rather than good; there is only one God. The Upanishads present a different way of fitting what had been popular religion into a sophisticated worldview. The gods and goddesses all are—if they are properly understood—aspects or personae of the single divine reality, Brahman. This is subtly accommodating to popular religion. The gods and goddesses can continue to be worshiped, but those in the know will be mindful that they are all aspects of Brahman.

Thus far I have been presenting the outlines of a worldview without giving the reasons for it. The reasons for identifying all gods and goddesses with Brahman will emerge when we look at the sources of the idea of *atman*. The link is that gods and goddesses, like human beings, have desires, aversions, and characteristic forms of behavior. In short they have personalities. The central argument underlying the metaphysics of the Upanishads is that personality has only a superficial kind of reality.

The best way of appreciating this view is to examine a persistent feature of human experience, sense of self. Most of us have a feeling, which is familiar but hard to analyze, that there is a "me" close to the surface of our normal experience. When we wake up in unfamiliar surroundings we may not know where we are, but there is the familiar "me." Usually we know who we are by name, but even in cases of amnesia there will be the "me" (although now it is more mysterious).

This "me" gives us a strong sense of ways in which actions and experience in a life—our life—are unified. It enables us to have immediate knowledge, not based on evidence, of connections. Sydney Shoemaker has given the example of knowing that it was I who broke the window yesterday. He points out that it would be over-simple to regard this knowledge as simply based on memory. Memory tells me that *someone* broke the window, but the claim that it was I requires the additional step of judging that I am identical with that person. Normally we do not need to look at videotape, or to consult eyewitnesses, in order to make this judgment.

What most people, quite possibly in every culture, firmly believe is that each of us has a "me" that persists through a life (and perhaps beyond) and that (in some sense) remains the same "me" throughout. This is intuitive and pre-philosophical. The obvious questions are "How do we know this?" and "What does this really mean?"

"How do we know this?" may be one of those questions that does not have a good answer. One thought is that we introspectively can take stock. We could look inside ourselves, that is, for something that looks like a "me," tracking it then as a stable element in our experience. The eighteenth-century Scottish philosopher David Hume tried this experiment and came up empty. This led him, in book 1 of his *Treatise of Human Nature,* to deny that any of us has a self, at least in the sense of a stable, unchanging element of our minds. More than two thousand years earlier, Buddha, reacting against a philosophical tradition that provided the base for what became known as Hinduism, tried the same experiment with the same result.

We need not conclude that the notion of a persistent and stable "me" is nonsense or is wrong. Perhaps the experiment of looking inward for a real self was miscast? Critics of Hume have sometimes asked, "If Hume looked for his self and failed to find it, what was doing the looking?" The difficulty of introspective search would seem to be that it is naturally "dualistic": that is, there is a separation between something looking and something looked for. But maybe a self, if there is one, includes both elements. Perhaps, then, a form of experience that is nondual, if such be possible, would be more successful?

Another alternative is that the self, rather than being an element of experience, is something posited in relation to all possible experience. This was the view of the eighteenth-century philosopher Immanuel Kant. He held that the self (at least the self connected with experience) is a unifying feature of the structure of experience and not something that could be an item within the structure.

The Upanishads offer an answer different from this, one that does appeal to a special kind of experience. Unlike Hume's introspection, this special kind of experience is not available to everyone. It requires extensive preparation and hard work. Its features are more easily explained if we first become clear about what the Upanishads mean by *atman,* and also how they are sure that it can be found if one searches for it in the proper way.

We have seen that there is a widespread assumption that each of us has a stable, persistent self. Can such a self change? Intuitively it might seem that the answer is "Yes." You are the same person you were a few years ago, even though undoubtedly you have changed in some respects. Reflective examination, though, undermines this intuitive confidence. We could imagine someone who is more like you were a few years ago than you now are. What then? The usual response is that, all the same, you (now) are you (then). Given continuous surveillance, we could have tracked you during the intervening period; and this continuity strengthens our sense of identity, even if the changes in you were in fact very great.

This line of thought would leave us with an identity that looks tempered by matters of degree. The ancient Greek philosopher Heraclitus is famous for the cryptic utterance "You can't step in the same river twice." What he presumably meant is that the river is constantly changing (different water flows through, there can be tiny variations in the positions of the river banks, etc.) so that, strictly speaking, today's river is not (entirely) the same as yesterday's river. In much the same spirit he might have argued that you can't be the same person today that you were yesterday. But a possible response is that we have conventions of language that enable rivers and persons to keep their names, and to count as the same by being pretty much the same.

These conventions usually work pretty well. But there are imaginable cases in which they start to break down. Some of these involve great change. If the river became very like what we would normally call a lake, that would put our sense of being confronted with the "same" river under considerable pressure. We could imagine cases in which someone's brain were entirely taken over by a terrible virus that had its own personality (and perhaps even its own name), in which there would be great hesitation in judging that what we were confronting is the same person we had known.

There also are imaginable cases in which what we might normally judge to be the same has close competitors that also might seem the same, thus introducing doubt. The Oxford philosopher Derek Parfit, in his *Reasons and Persons,* has given a nice example of this. He imagines your traveling to Mars by Teletransporter. This process involves going to a room on Earth and pressing a green button. You lose consciousness; all your cells are destroyed on Earth, and at the same time you are reassembled on Mars. After you have made several trips this way, there is one in which there is a malfunctioning of the apparatus. You regain consciousness on Earth but now there is also a you on Mars. This duplication might seem to create problems, but an attendant assures you that the you still on Earth will within a short time suffer cardiac arrest. (So, not to worry!?)

This hypothetical case raises questions of whether either or both of the you's in this story can be considered identical to the old you.

Also, do the previous instances of Teletransportation count as cases in which a you on Mars was identical to the you that had been on Earth? Or were these cases in which death on Earth was combined with duplication on Mars (i.e., a new person on Mars who was, as it were, a xerox copy of the old you on Earth)?

Parfit throughout his book devises a variety of ingenious cases in which—despite our conventions of what counts as the same person—we have trouble in deciding what to say. We might have assumed that questions of "Is it me?" in general have an objective "Yes" or "No" answer. But Parfit's examples are not like this.

All of this exploration does not exactly prove that you cannot both hold that you have a persistent "me," and at the same time accept that this "me" continually changes. But it does place the combination under argumentative pressure. There may be cases in which there is not a straightforward right answer, especially if there is a competing candidate to count as "you," or if the changes are very great.

Despite this, our intuitive sense of having a persistent "me" is hardly the sense of having one that is largely the same as yesterday's me, or pretty much the same as last year's. Rather we tend to assume that the "me" that persists through a lifetime has an identity that, as the eighteenth-century philosopher Bishop Butler put it, is "strict and philosophical" rather than "loose and popular." You are you, period—not 90 percent you, not 99 percent you—but simply you.

Most contemporary philosophers who work on problems of the self have come to think (largely on the basis of arguments like those just referred to) that this is indefensible. You have a self, in their view, only in a conventional sense governed by our criteria for what counts as the "same" person. There are interesting and positive things to be said about how such a "self" is developed. Hume, the pioneer in Western philosophy of this line of thought, explores it at length in book 2 of his *Treatise of Human Nature*.

There is an alternative response, though. One might simply deny that the persistent "me" changes. Personality, the thoughts and feelings we have, and our physical appearance all change. But perhaps there is something underlying all of these things, some core of our being, that does not change?

The late-twentieth-century philosopher Roderick Chisholm, in his *Person and Object*, suggested such a view: that each of us has an inner self-nature, a "haecceity," which is available to introspective experience. This suggestion (which Chisholm later appeared to drop) had the appeal of having it both ways, preserving individuality (everyone's haecceity is different from everyone else's) while insisting on changelessness. However, there was the difficulty that our experiences of individuality are all bound up with things, including our thoughts and styles of behavior, that do change.

There is one alternative remaining, if we want to do justice to our intuitive sense of an unchanging "me" throughout life. This is to look for a core of self that has no elements of individual natures that grow and change. This would be a core that underlies (and is separate from) personality, thought patterns, bodily nature, and so forth.

This is *atman*. In the view of the Upanishads, this is what, at the deepest level, you are.

What I am suggesting is that the Upanishads' view of *atman* makes good philosophical sense if it is seen as the conclusion of the following (largely implicit) argument.

> Each of us has a persistent "me."
>
> This "me" (as it intuitively seems) must be unchanging.
>
> But personality, thought patterns, and so on, do change.
>
> Therefore the persistent "me" cannot include such elements.

The further conclusion is that your persistent "me," lacking all elements of individuality, is the same as anyone else's persistent "me." Once individuality is subtracted, what is there to distinguish you (qualitatively) from anyone else? The Upanishads indeed assume something broader: that the inner nature of all things, and not merely of all conscious beings, will be the same. This yields an image of the universe as a field of inner realities that are all at bottom the same. The inner realities of gods and goddesses, once their individualities are discounted, are included in this. The name for this field of inner realities is Brahman. *Atman,* then, is Brahman in somewhat the way in which a drop of water is the ocean of which it is a part. Whether the identity of *atman* and Brahman should be viewed straightforwardly as a matter of the same thing in two different guises, or as an identity between part and whole, becomes a debatable subject in Hindu philosophy.

Some Implications

The religious implication of this philosophy is that folk polytheism is not repudiated or scorned. But there is a higher interpretation in which what is worshiped is always in fact a single divine reality, which takes the diverse forms of the traditional gods and goddesses. We also are parts of that single divine reality, which in the drama of the universe plays the part of you (and indeed plays all the parts, as well as being the scenery). Someone who accepts the Upanishads can say "I am God," which in Christianity, Judaism, and Islam would be considered heretical and blasphemous, but in the intellectual forms of Hinduism would be taken for granted.

The philosophical implications of the identity of *atman* and Brahman are far more complicated. They include a philosophical monism—the entire universe is one thing—which is what would remind some readers of Spinoza. But they include also an account of what we are that is more complex and qualified than one might at first think.

There is the sense, of course, in which (if the Upanishads are right) you never change: Brahman is always Brahman. But, on the other hand, there are obvious respects in which you *do* change, especially as you come to think of yourself as Brahman.

There also is the problem of the layers of individual personality that surround the *atman*. According to the Upanishads, they are not the real you or any part of the real you. But all the same they are there, and the Upanishads talk about the importance of seeing beneath them (and perhaps, to a degree, getting rid of them).

Are these individualistic elements of personality Brahman? If they are, then what is so special about *atman*? If they are not, then it cannot be true that the entire universe is Brahman.

These difficulties about the status of your individual personality are peculiarly philosophical, not least in the way in which one hardly knows what to say. We need to put them aside for a little while. We can become clearer about them if we first investigate what is supposed to happen after you begin to think you have, underneath the layers of individual personality, an *atman*.

The Search for *Atman*

Including your *atman* in your knowledge is not easy, but it is required both for enlightenment and for liberation. If philosophical Hinduism were like some forms of religion we might be familiar with, then all you would have to do is say sincerely "I've got an *atman* and it's Brahman" and (assuming that you are also a moral person) you would be saved. The Upanishads make it clear that this is not true. What *will* make a difference to the quality of your life (and solve Nachiketas's worry about death) is if you come thoroughly to think in terms of *atman* as Brahman. This requires, among other things, a clear experiential sense of your *atman*. Merely an abstract formulation will not do.

There is a huge difference between believing something, more or less, and thoroughly thinking in terms of it. Imagine this case. Bloggs sincerely believes (he could pass a lie detector test on this) that there is life after death, including the possibility of a heaven that is far more gratifying than life here on earth. He also believes that his chances for heaven are good, and indeed at present are as good as they are ever likely to be. Someone then says to him, "Good news, Bloggs. You are going to die in the next five minutes." Bloggs will be happy, right?

Well he may be. But it seems likely that many genuinely religious people would not be. What is relevant is the extent to which an idea, or a set of ideas, engrosses one's mind. The Upanishads clearly assume that the metaphysical claim *"atman* is Brahman" generates an ethical imperative. One should take steps to change one's moment-to-moment thinking so that it is entirely engrossed by the idea that *atman* is Brahman. This process is facilitated by prolonged experiential contact with the nature of one's *atman*.

Clearly yoga, which in ancient Sanskrit simply means "technique," is important in this search. Someone who wishes to encounter the core of her or his being, underneath layers of changing personality, needs to have a steady mind, one that does not wander. Physical techniques that steady and calm bodily impulses can make a difference. Quiet surroundings with few distractions can help.

The evidence suggests that the Upanishads gave rise to cultural practices in which some members of the upper castes (who were thought to be the only ones ready for enlightenment, at least in this lifetime) devoted themselves to meditative search for their *atmans*. Sometimes people would begin this in their youth, but there also was a pattern in which people led normal family lives to the point at which their children were grown, and then—at the stage at which in our society they might begin to think about retirement communities—they would withdraw from normal life and spend their lives in remote locations seeking spiritual enlightenment. To the outside observer they might appear half-starved and withdrawn. This behavior on the part of members of the privileged classes is an ironic commentary on the idea found in the crudest ("vulgar") forms of Marxism that religious ideas are expressions of what is in the interests of the dominant classes, although in a way someone who accepts the Upanishads might think that there was a class interest in spiritual liberation.

On one persistent interpretation in Hindu philosophy, the experience of *atman* would have to be nondual. That is, it would not be a matter of the meditator scrutinizing something psychic and saying "aha, this is *atman*." Rather there would be a state of experience in which there was no separation between the knower and the known, no polarization within the experience. Indeed, the experience would have to be oddly featureless, but very calm. More than one of the Upanishads insists that it would be totally unlike normal waking experience or dreaming, but rather more like dreamless sleep (although not entirely the same). Presumably, then, any identification of *atman* would be after the experience, and not within it.

It should be emphasized here that there is great variety in Hindu philosophy, and one should not assume more consensus than there is in Western philosophy. What I am presenting here is what seems to me a dominant and compelling interpretation of the Upanishads.

It cannot too strongly be emphasized also that what the Upanishads ask for is extremely difficult, making it very unlikely that more than a small number of people in any generation would be entirely successful. Experiential knowledge of *atman* and coming entirely to think in terms of its identity with Brahman would have to be a full-time job. It would require an extreme preoccupation with one's inner nature that accentuates the introspective turn so prominent in Indian culture, and which distresses some writers (notably V. S. Naipaul in *India, A Wounded Civilization*) whose roots are in Indian culture.

Someone whose thinking is entirely engrossed by the view that *atman* is Brahman presumably would no longer draw any boundaries within the world, and would not know her or his own name. One irony is that, while such a person would have reached enlightenment, the notion that she or he had reached enlightenment would seem (to that person) entirely meaningless. Indeed, the very desire to attain enlightenment, which had to get the difficult process starting, would have faded away (along with all other desires) well before the final victory. The individual's enlightenment, in short, would seem real from the outside—from the point of view of those who still think of the world in terms of distinct individuals and are not enlightened—but not from the inside.

It is time to say more about the emotions of the path to enlightenment, and specifically of pleasure and joy. Why is pleasure considered a trap? Any answer must consider the variety of things that are labeled "pleasure," and what many of them have in common. A great many sensory gratifications count as pleasures, including the obvious examples of food, drink, and sex, along with less obvious examples of bodily relaxation and of relief from discomfort. Seeing good friends is a pleasure, as is the thought that one has nothing to reproach oneself with. For someone who enjoys mathematics, an elegant proof can provide pleasure.

It should be clear that pleasures are very diverse, but that they typically are keyed to something that produces them. The something can be an object, an experience, or a thought. A natural thought is that the value of a pleasure will depend on, among other things, what it is keyed to. The value of the pleasure afforded by an extremely subtle and exquisite experience might seem to exceed that afforded by a warm shower on a cold day. We might not know what to say about the pleasure of activities that we judge less than worthless. What value does the pleasure of the sadist, after a good day in the torture chamber, have?

One of the general characteristics of pleasures, despite the great diversity, is that they tend to be brief. This is part of the contrast with happiness. We do, it is true, speak of being happy about something, perhaps something that happens to us; and such feelings or moods, keyed as they are to an occasion, can be brief. But there is also a sense in which someone can be happy, period—without the happiness being about anything specific. Such "global" happiness can go on for weeks, months, or an entire life. Pleasure, keyed as it is to things that come and go, cannot be indefinitely prolonged, and must be renewed. Another contrast between pleasure and global happiness is that, according to some psychologists, global happiness requires a high degree of self-acceptance. That is, you can't be happy (in this sense) unless you basically like yourself. Pleasure, on the other hand, seems to depend mainly on whatever it is, outside the self, that it is keyed to.

An obvious problem with pleasure, then, is that caring about it has an element of built-in vulnerability. The world outside of us may not provide what we want. There is a more subtle problem. It can be argued that pleasures often require periods of prior frustration if they are to seem at all intense or meaningful, and also that they are addictive. If we get the pleasure we want—the argument goes—it is just a matter of time before we want more (or perhaps some different pleasures). This after-pleasure interval is marked by an increasing sense of boredom. Hence, there is a cycle in which the pleasure is paid for in advance by frustration and is paid for again in boredom. And this is in the favorable case, the one in which we actually get the pleasure. Sometimes we pay in frustration and then get nothing.

A simple example of the frustration-pleasure link is this: you could come to get intense pleasure from a simple glass of water. It is easy: just don't have anything to drink for the next couple of days, and then you will be amazed at how pleasant the glass of water is. Perhaps some of the sensual pleasures that people most look forward to would seem less interesting—in the way that glasses of water do to us—in a parallel universe of instant gratification?

There has been considerable cross-cultural awareness of this downside of pleasures. Is it true for all pleasures? Perhaps the role of prior frustration is less marked in the cases of the pleasure of being with friends, or of enjoying the elegant proof in mathematics, than it is in the case of purely sensory pleasures? Something like this seems to have been the thought of the ancient Greek philosopher Epicurus, who (despite the misleading associations that the word "epicurean" has acquired) recommended a strategy in life that emphasized pleasures such as those of the companionship of friends and downplayed sensory pleasures. A deliberately simple life, he contended, would minimize pain.

Clearly, from the point of view of the Upanishads, pleasures of all sorts (but especially of the kinds eschewed by Epicurus) have multiple disadvantages. They are distracting. Once people get hooked on them, they think about them a great deal. They tend to be inherently outward-focusing, providing an emphasis on the possible sources of satisfaction. Pleasures lead to emotional waves of desire and frustration, with some mixture perhaps of recollected gratification, which must spoil the calm needed in the search for *atman*.

Joy is harder than pleasure to talk about. For one thing, it is a much less common part of life for most of us. Also, it is easier to talk about an emotional experience if you can refer to a common "objective correlative": that is, refer to the kind of thing in the presence of which the emotional experience often occurs. Good food, sex, meetings with greatly missed friends, and so forth, all provide ready ways of talking about pleasure. But joy seems much less predictable than pleasure is, and it is far harder to think of regular occasions of joy.

Joy is like happiness in one respect. We do speak sometimes of joy in relation to specific things and occurrences. Much as we are happy about this or that, we also say that such and such gives me joy. A young child or a personal achievement can give someone joy in this sense.

Alongside this object-keyed sense, there is one in which joy simply comes; it is not about anything in particular. The poet, standing in a field of daffodils, can be surprised by joy. The joy scarcely is *in* the daffodils. They are the almost accidental setting for something that comes from inside. Besides "global" happiness we can speak of global (objectless) joy. This is the joy that is praised by the Upanishads.

It is easier to say this much about joy than it is to specify why and when it arises. Why is there so little joy in the daily lives of most of us? Is it that we have so many concerns? If we look for people who do seem from time to time to experience joy, the best examples are small children, and perhaps also adults living simple lives in difficult circumstances. Calcutta, a city of incredible poverty, has been termed a "city of joy," something that would be unlikely to be said of a prosperous center of business activity.

One thought is that our development after early childhood consists to a large degree of emotional cocooning, protecting ourselves from the sharp emotions (both negative and positive) of small children, and also insulating ourselves from the rawness of the world. Perhaps suffering, as in the case of the poet who was finally surprised by joy, rips away the cocoon?

If this were the whole story, then it would appear that (at least in some cases) joy is like pleasure in being a poor bargain: in itself it is valued, but the advance payment is proportionally steep. However, I do not think that this is what the Upanishads have in mind. The path to enlightenment that they recommend is difficult, in terms of the effort required and the disruption of ordinary life. But there is no suggestion that it is painful or that one suffers.

The crucial features of joy in their view might seem to be the following: (1) Joy comes from inside and in that sense is not dependent on occasions and circumstances. (2) Joy comes from a psychic life that is uncluttered and therefore relatively open. (3) In some cases joy is related to a sense of well-functioning in this psychic life. To be in tune with the world, so to speak, can be a source of joy.

This concept of joy makes it understandable that the Upanishads view the search for enlightenment as a path that, without requiring antecedent suffering, will lead to predictable joy. The quiet inner satisfaction of the mystic who is nearly there could be intense and very rewarding. The emotional trade-off is that you give up pleasure, with its distractions and risks, for something in the end that is much greater and more predictable.

The World of Superficial Reality

We need to return to the question of what kind of reality individual personality has. The negative judgment on it by now should be apparent. Your individual personality is not really you. The real you, which never changes, is *atman,* which is identical with Brahman (which also never changes).

Are the outer layers of individual personality, which surround your *atman,* then an illusion? They certainly are not a *delusion*: that is, they are not like introspective hallucinations that have no footing in the world as it really is. An illusion, as opposed to a delusion, is something that distorts a reality that is there (but in a different form from the one that you take it to have). In this sense, the Upanishads do hold that individual personality is an illusion.

Nevertheless, it is an illusion that has an experiential life of its own. One of the striking things about the progress to enlightenment, though, is that the experiential life of individual personality is more ample and noticeable at the beginning than it is toward the end. Ancient Hindu texts convey a sense that to be enlightened or nearly enlightened is to be highly impersonal in affect, manner, and self-presentation. It is as if the layers of individual personality, once seen through, also begin to fade away. When you have seen one enlightened person, you have seen them all.

It sometimes seems as if the Upanishads want to say two divergent things at the same time. One is that there is a sense in which to become enlightened, fully engrossed in the mode of thought that goes along with the claim that *atman* is Brahman, is to become Brahman. Certainly the person on the way to enlightenment becomes more Brahman-ish, losing personality characteristics that might look as if they distinguish a person from the rest of the universe. But the Upanishads clearly insist that such a person (like all of us) always was Brahman. Everything is Brahman.

Along this line there are clear statements that individual personality characteristics are parts of the reality that Brahman spins out of itself, creating the universe out of itself like a spider spinning a web. If our atman is Brahman, then these personality characteristics also are Brahman. Are they equally Brahman? A recurrent metaphor is that each of us is like a drop of water in the ocean that is Brahman. Perhaps the individual personality characteristics could be compared to froth surrounding the drops of water?

The puzzle here should be related to a set of puzzling characteristics of the general Hindu thought system in which the Upanishads play a central role. On one hand, both the ideal presented by the Upanishads and the reality it claims is fundamental are highly impersonal. We all are one. On the other hand, the social reality that Hinduism (before fairly recently) endorsed hardly treats all humans as one, and indeed takes caste distinctions very seriously.

It might be held that all religions as actually practiced, and perhaps all great systems of thought in general, have internal contradictions. The pulls and counterpulls can be part of the fascination and the tension of the system of thought. The Upanishads, though, may be a special case. They are unusually philosophically self-conscious texts. There is a consistent tendency also to describe the universe both as Brahman and at the same time in more specific terms keyed to individual realities. This consistency makes me think that there is actually *not* an internal contradiction. If there were, it would have been too obvious to everyone concerned.

Here is an analogy that may be helpful. The scientist and philosopher Sir Arthur Eddington, in the introduction to his *The Nature of the Physical World,* remarks that the table in front of him is in a way two tables. One is the solid and dense table of common sense. The other is the largely empty table of nuclear physics, with elementary particles moving about. This allows the formulation of true statements that on the surface appear incompatible with one another. It is true (in the framework of common sense) that the table is solid and dense. It also is true (in the framework of nuclear physics) that it is largely empty space.

Some people, of course, would want to insist that there is only one system of truth. One option might be to reject nuclear physics utterly, or alternatively to regard it as a kind of mythic structure whose true meanings are to be found only in ordinary experience. Alternatively one might flatly reject the commonsense picture of the world as prescientific or as "folk science."

Both of these simplifications have real difficulties. Rejecting nuclear physics of course would be stupid. It is far from clear, though, that we can do justice to its meanings, and to the quality of the evidence to which it appeals, if we regard it as merely a mythic superstructure that can be "cashed" in ordinary experience. Conversely, by ordinary criteria the table in front of Eddington (as distinguished from one that was in fact hollow) presumably *was* solid and dense.

A basic philosophical point is that one cannot separate sharply what is meant by calling a statement "true" from acceptable criteria for judging that it is true. There are acceptable criteria within the framework of nuclear physics for judging that the table was largely empty space. There also were acceptable criteria for judging that it was solid and dense.

So it looks highly plausible to hold that there genuinely can be two different sets of statements that provide a picture of something real (e.g., a table), that both can count as true even if the pictures they provide are very different. We can accept this without necessarily holding that the two sets of statements are on a par. We can consistently claim that, say, the statements of nuclear physics present a deeper truth than those of common sense.

In much this spirit, we can take the Upanishads to be presenting two different frameworks within which what is real can be understood and described. What is thought of as the deeper truth is provided by the framework that is informed by *"atman* is Brahman." In this framework there is only one reality, Brahman. Everything is Brahman, and nothing ever changes.

Let us call this framework Ultimate Reality. There is also a framework of Superficial Reality, which represents the view of anyone whose thinking has not been entirely engrossed by the idea that *atman* is Brahman. In this framework there are countless individuals, including humans, animals, plants, pieces of furniture, gods and goddesses. Each of these things has its own characteristics. There is change, including processes of creation, preservation, destruction, life and death, spiritual fulfillment, spiritual sloth, and outright sin.

It is important to the Upanishads that there are truths within the framework of Superficial Reality. The phrase "superficial reality" may sound belittling, but anyone who writes a book, for which it is expected there will be readers, is (from the point of view of the authors of the Upanishads) operating within a framework of superficial reality. People who are fully enlightened do not write books. It is highly doubtful that they even know who (as individuals) they are or that there are differences between them and other people.

Conclusion

The Upanishads begin, both theoretically and practically, with self. The true self of the reader is put in question: it cannot be the individual personality, because one wakes up every morning recognizing oneself as the same person, and it would be hard to account for the precision and certainty of that knowledge given the changeable nature of individual personality. Thus we can find the true nature of who we are only by meditating beneath the surface of everything individual. This leads us to *atman*. Encountering *atman* saves the theory that everyone has an unchanging self, but it also is a first step toward personal liberation.

The full world picture of the Upanishads has been argued to be really a split screen. The deepest truth is that, because *atman* is Brahman, everything is Brahman. The entire universe is a single divine reality, which never really changes. On the other side of the split screen, we can see a universe full of individual things and beings that are constantly changing. In the view of the Upanishads it is true that some humans have more immediate spiritual potential than others do. The former are urged to want to allow the vision of *atman* as Brahman to engross their thinking, which will lead them to joy and to a spiritual achievement that will preclude any further reincarnations. In the process of this achievement, they will care less and less about the goal. When the idea of being a liberated individual comes to seem entirely meaningless, they will have arrived.

Recommended Reading

J. N. Mohanty, "A History of Indian Philosophy," in *A Companion to World Philosophies,* ed. Eliot Deutsch and Ron Bontekoe (Oxford: Blackwell, 1997), 24–48. Mohanty gives a very good overview of the subject.

Surendranath Dasgupta, *Indian Idealism* (Cambridge: Cambridge University Press, 1962). This is a beautifully written book. The chapters on the Upanishads are exceptionally clear.

Eliot Deutsch, *Advaita Vedanta* (Honolulu: University Press of Hawaii, 1969) This also is an excellent, exceptionally clear book, devoted to a major school of Indian philosophy derived from the Upanishads, one in which the great Samkara (ca. 800 C.E.) is a central figure.

Two books that will give a reader a good sense of recent Western philosophy on issues of personal identity and selfhood are *Personal Identity,* ed. John Perry (Berkeley: University of California Press, 1975), and John Perry, *A Dialogue on Personal Identity and Immortality* (Indianapolis: Hackett, 1978). The first book is a collection of essays by major philosophers, including the one by Sydney Shoemaker referred to in this chapter. Perry's *Dialogue* is a fine example of a highly sophisticated philosopher examining important issues in a clear, concise, and untechnical way, simplifying but not oversimplifying. Those who have no philosophical background will find it highly readable.

TWO

THE DHAMMAPADA

If the central thesis of the Upanishads is easy to summarize (*atman* is Brahman), so also is the central claim of early Buddhist philosophy. It is *anatman:* there is no *atman.* The Dhammapada centers a picture of what we are like, and of what the world is like, on this claim.

This metaphysics is opposite to that of Hindu philosophy. Where the Upanishads sees the world as most profoundly a unity, Buddhist philosophy sees it as a swirl of fragments, linked by causal relations and by other associations. Not only is there no *atman,* there also is no Brahman. The two traditions share a scorn of egoism and individualism. But the grounds are very different. In the view of the Upanishads, there are no differences among individuals in ultimate reality, because there really are no individuals. The Buddhist view is that there are differences, but (understood properly) they are largely matters of convention and are unimportant.

The structure of the Dhammapada is like that of the Upanishads in linking two elements of philosophy. There is the metaphysics, but even more prominent is an ethics that is supposed to flow from the metaphysics. In the Dhammapada, ethics really predominates. The ways in which the ethics of the Dhammapada departs from that of the Upanishads are best appreciated if we begin by looking at the popular presentation of Buddhism as a movement.

Buddha's Compassion

The man known as the Buddha was a real human being. We know that he was born in an aristocratic family in the northernmost region of the Indian cultural zone (in what is now Nepal) in the middle of the sixth century BCE. This makes him a contemporary of Confucius in China, a century before the birth of Socrates in Greece. By the time of Buddha's birth there were many varieties of rootless ascetics, some of them eating very little food and absorbed in meditation, who were dedicated to engrossing their consciousness in ultimate spiritual truth.

This much is fact. It is surrounded by popular legends of Buddha's birth and early history. According to these, Buddha's parents had been warned at his birth that he would become a holy man. This would mean in effect that he would be lost to his family, so (according to the legends) they took steps to shield the young Buddha from the experiences that might impel him in a religious direction. He had every comfort, but was not exposed to the dark elements of human life, such as sickness, old age, and death. He married young and had a son.

The gods, as the legends have it, did want Buddha to be a holy man. Their role in the story actually is minimal, just as their role in Buddhism—as it took form as a popular religion—is negligible. The early Buddhist story was that the gods are like us in having desires, worries, and uncertainties about the direction of life. This is why they wanted Buddha to become a holy man: they anticipated that he would come up with solutions to the problems of life that would be helpful to them, as well as to us human beings.

The role of the gods in the legends is that they miraculously expose Buddha to experiences that shock him, and that awaken his religious vocation. One day he sees someone who is very sick. Subsequently he sees someone who is old, and he sees a corpse. Finally, in contrast, he sees an ascetic in a blissful state. He realizes that ordinary life is not idyllic as he had thought, and that suffering (especially given the inevitability of sickness, old age, and death) is deeply woven into it. He takes on the mission of coming up with a solution to the problem of suffering that not only will protect him but also can be taught to others.

This is Buddha's compassion. Most readers will see the legends of Buddha's early life as sheer fantasy, but these legends do dramatize something that is real and is unique to Buddhism. Traditional Hinduism, like other major religions, provided ample room for kindness and charity. But the view of suffering that followed from the basic religious assumptions was that it was a natural part of life, often the result of poor karma that stemmed from misdeeds in a previous life. In any event, one could look beyond current suffering to prospects in future reincarnations.

If one looks more widely at religious traditions, one sees that in the Old Testament the Book of Job suggests that suffering is to a degree an unforeseeable contingency of life: one might appeal to God's justice, but this is far beyond human justice and cannot be understood by us. Suffering is at the heart of the New Testament narrative, in the form of the crucifixion. The notion of taking up one's cross and following Jesus suggests that suffering can be made into a deep spiritual experience.

The legends of Buddha's early life capture the truth that Buddha was disturbed by suffering in an unparalleled way: he wanted to eliminate it. The ideal was a life, or an entire world, without suffering. This concern underlies the metaphysics and the ethics. It also plays a decisive role in the mission. In the world of the Upanishads, to be fully enlightened was to be free of the ordinary vision of reality, and thereby to be out of communication with ordinary human beings. Buddha's quest was for total enlightenment that permitted teaching, that allowed him to share his knowledge with other people.

Other legends dramatize the fact that Buddha's concern was for all suffering, with no line drawn between humans and animals. There is a charming book of stories, *The Jataka Tales,* of previous lives of the being who finally was reincarnated as Gautama, the man who became known as the Buddha. Some of these previous lives were as an animal. Buddha once was an elephant (but a very good elephant!). He was once a hare, who sacrificed his life for others. There is a later story (included in Edward Conze's *Buddhist Scriptures*) of a previous life as a human being, in which the man who would become Gautama/the Buddha encountered a starving tigress and her cubs. They urgently needed food to end their suffering and to survive, and he considerately offered himself. But the tigress was too feeble to come to chew on him, so he approached her and helped her by cutting himself (making himself appetizingly bloody) and falling down near her.

All of this is folktale, but it points to a truth about Buddha's orientation. The legends of his early life describe him, once he decides to take on the mission of solving the problem of suffering, as leaving his family (including his wife and young son). He joins wandering ascetics, and like them starves himself and meditates. He becomes so thin that his backbone and belly button are hardly separate. But none of this gives him what he wants.

If this traditional approach fails for Buddha, it is partly because his goals are different from those of the others. They merely are looking for personal salvation. He is looking for something that goes beyond any private adjustment of vision: he needs something rationally formulatable so that it can be communicated to others. Building up his strength for this, Buddha has a decent meal, and then meditates beneath a tree until he finally comes up with the solution to the problem of suffering.

Before we look at his solution, it is worth noting one lesson that Buddha took from his experiences on the road to enlightenment. It was the repudiation of extreme asceticism. Many readers may have heard of Buddha's "Middle Way," which might sound (misleadingly) like a general policy of moderation. Buddha's views on some issues, as we will see, were not by most standards middle of the road. The "Middle Way" broadly includes the Eightfold Path (right views, right intentions, etc.), which is the entire Buddhist approach to life. More narrowly it concerns things such as food. The idea here is that food should not be important, either positively or (as in extreme asceticism) negatively. Statues of Buddha as he got older sometimes depict him as somewhat plump. The idea is that a wandering monk should take food as it is offered, and not care whether it is especially tasty or very much the opposite. This is part of a general policy of increasing detachment.

The Cause of Suffering

If suffering is a disease, then of course one needs to understand the cause in order to find a cure. The Dhammapada is built around a complicated diagnosis. The *proximate* cause of suffering is the human phenomenon of desire, which becomes addictive and guarantees suffering. But this too has its cause. The *ultimate* cause of desire and suffering is a mistaken view of the self.

The characterization of the self provided in the Dhammapada is concise, so concise indeed that many readers might not recognize part of the point. It occurs in the Twin Verses at the very beginning. In the translation by S. Radhakrishnan for Oxford University Press these verses include "(The mental) natures are the result of what we have thought, are chieftained by our thoughts, are made up of our thoughts." Juan Mascaro's translation (Penguin) has "What we are today comes from our thoughts of yesterday, and our present thoughts build our life of tomorrow: our life is the creation of our mind."

An obvious reading is that what we think (or allow ourselves to think) determines the shape in which our personality develops. Clearly this is part of the early Buddhist message. Thought control, that is, control of one's own thinking, is taken seriously as part of the regimen of becoming enlightened. But there is also a claim about what is being shaped that must be taken literally. What we are *is* what we have thought or are thinking. There is nothing more to us than that.

Much of the force of this claim obtains because of the implicit rejection of the *atman* of the Upanishads. There is no unchanging *atman* that is us, such that our thoughts provide a mere surrounding of our true nature. But even someone who never had read the Upanishads might find something disturbing in the literal meaning of the Twin Verses. There is a common tendency, especially when what we are thinking seems unworthy or embarrassing, to find reassurance in the notion of a "real me" that is better than the current contents of the mind. Someone who accepts the Dhammapada could agree that a person's thinking can vary, and that thoughts at any given moment need not represent the dominant tendencies of the system of thoughts that is the person. Nevertheless, in the early Buddhist view, no one has a "real me" apart from the system of thoughts. In that sense, you are what you think.

The Dhammapada is an exceptionally accessible piece of philosophical writing in part because its arguments are not fully spelled out, and remain largely implicit. There also is not the worrying over qualifications and complications that is characteristic of much philosophical investigation. Much of this complication, in relation to the self, emerges to view in another early Buddhist classic, *The Questions of King Milinda*. This work includes long stretches of probing philosophical dialogue on the nature of the self.

The problem is, as was the case for the Upanishads, that an anti-individualistic metaphysics may need to account for the way our ordinary thought and discourse is built around the recognition of individual personalities. The Upanishads (to review briefly) are anti-individualistic in that everything that makes someone a distinct individual is argued to be an illusion: we are all Brahman. But the individualism of our ordinary thought and discourse remains present as the less-regarded half of a split-screen view of reality. It has validity within the framework of superficial truths.

The Dhammapada is anti-individualistic in that contents of the system of thoughts that is you are almost fortuitously part of you rather than someone else. The boundaries between your system and someone else's come to look fairly arbitrary. There is no essence of self that could determine a really firm boundary. That person's suffering from an unpleasant disease could just as well have been yours.

Nevertheless, we do recognize individuals, including the Buddha, by names. And even an enlightened person might have some sense of an individual identity and a personal identity. The Buddha claimed to have attained nirvana (the Buddhist form of final spiritual release, comparable to the Hindu *moksha*) while still alive. Yet he was still talking to people, and presumably knew his name.

The Questions of King Milinda addresses this issue of individual identity. One might compare a person to a chariot, and in terms of this analogy ask where the self of the person could be located. A tempting answer might be that the self is a key determining element of a person. But the chariot cannot be identified with any of its parts, or any item in what one might experience of the chariot (vol. 1, pp. 63–64). Similarly the self of ordinary discourse is not an item of experience, not even an item (such as the *atman* of the Upanishads) that requires unusual skill and preparation to be in touch with. Rather (like the chariot) it is the system of parts or elements. Buddha's view, like that of David Hume more than two thousand years later, was that the self that we can meaningfully talk about must be seen as a bundle of psychic elements. Hume scholars, such as Annette Baier, have pointed out that there is a major difference between a bundle and a heap. The self of ordinary discourse may well have a degree of coherence and unity. Connections among the thoughts and feelings that help to make it up will be provided by such things as memories, habits, and plans.

Nevertheless, there remains something seemingly fortuitous about the boundaries. This is best seen in early Buddhist philosophy in relation to the topic of reincarnation. Popular Buddhism shared with Hinduism a firm belief in, and preoccupation with, reincarnation. We have already noted that the *Jataka Tales* told stories about previous lives of the Buddha. Throughout the transformations of Buddhism in South Asia and in China, Korea, and Japan, most forms have included beliefs in reincarnation. This belief works its way into popular consciousness in a variety of ways. The final chapter of the great Chinese novel (ca. 1600) *The Golden Lotus,* for example, tells (as many Western novels do) what happens in the end to some of its characters. But this account includes the forms in which some of them are reincarnated.

So much for popular Buddhism. The philosophy of early Buddhism can be far less straightforward on this point. We have seen that your self is a bundle of thoughts, feelings, urges, and the like. As new thoughts, feelings, and desires occur, the nature of the bundle keeps changing. What makes you, then, the same person throughout your life? Presumably the continuity provided by memories and the like, along with continuing similarities in personality, will be part of the answer. There also is the fact of bodily continuity, as might be reviewed by a continuous videotape of your entire life. Even if your personality changes, and you forget everything, the fact of bodily continuity will anchor the assumption of continuing personal identity.

This fact is absent from any supposed cases of reincarnation. Thus one might expect Buddhist philosophers to ask, as the writers of the Upanishads did not, what makes the infant who is the alleged reincarnation of X (who just died) the same person as X. This looks like a difficult question, in which the criteria that we apply within a single lifetime do not seem necessarily decisive.

My inclination is to think that the Upanishads do have ample room for an answer to this question. Even if each of us as an *atman* is, within the framework of ultimate reality, qualitatively the same as anyone else as an *atman*—like drops of water in a spiritual ocean—still it would be in theory possible for a being with complete access to the realm of superficial reality, and extraordinary powers of observation, to track the path of one spiritual drop as opposed to another. Your *atman* of course remains *atman* after the death of the individual you, but it could (in theory) be tracked into a life in which it is surrounded by a different individual personality and identity. The deepest truth remains that nothing happens at all: Brahman remains Brahman. But within a framework of superficial reality, it can be true that your *atman* enters a new individual life.

This story is not available to Buddhist philosophers. They deny the existence of an *atman*. What they are left with is a set of similarities or continuities that the infant who just has been born may have with X who just died. This is much like what we might have in the case of an older person who is perhaps the same as someone we used to know (whom we have not seen for a while), except that the crucial element of bodily continuity is missing (and also there are very likely to be fewer or no memories).

It is sometimes assumed in popular Buddhism that there may be a few vague memories of a previous life. This is said to play a part in the determination of the boy who will be the new Dalai Lama after the old one has died. The winning candidate will be a boy of the right age who seems to remember a few of the details of the life of the old Dalai Lama. Even if this idea is accepted, how can we distinguish between memories of things that predate one's birth, on one hand, and, on the other, something like thought broadcasts from the past? In the former case, we mysteriously might be presumed to be the same person who had the original experiences. In the latter case we are a different person who mysteriously has access to some of these original experiences. Both of the possible interpretations of the seeming-memories go well beyond anything in our ordinary sense of what the real world is like. Is there any way to choose between them?

The Questions of King Milinda in effect leaves room for an answer of "No." It does this while accommodating the eagerness of popular Buddhism to think in terms of reincarnation. Indeed, the way in which the philosophical account differs greatly from popular views, while not rejecting them, may be reminiscent of the relation between the Upanishads and popular Hinduism.

The main line of argument is this. People constantly change. King Milinda asks his Buddhist teacher whether someone who is born remains (in this life) the same or becomes other. The answer (vol. 1, p. 63) is neither, but that we can group together all of the changing states because of the continuity of the body. The analogy is with a changing flame, which, however, continues to be on the same lamp. To be reincarnated, then, is like the flame of one lamp being used to light a flame on another lamp. The factor of bodily continuity is now missing. Is the flame on the second lamp *the same* as that on the first lamp, or is it a different flame?

The obvious reply would be that you can say what you like. Our ordinary criteria for what we are willing to speak of as "the same" do not render a clear decision in this case. Equally, the ordinary criteria for "same person," which work smoothly in most ordinary cases, do not render as clear a verdict in the case of putative reincarnation. Nevertheless, if we accept psychic continuity from one life to another, we *could* speak of reincarnation.

The ordinary Buddhist thus can see the flow of life in the world in terms of reincarnation without running directly counter to anything in philosophical Buddhism. But the philosophical Buddhist knows that there is no *atman* that is transmitted from one life to the next. Reincarnation is not rejected—one can see the world in that way—but there will be an ironic distance.

This is linked to the central point. The widespread human assumption that one has an inner self, which remains the same throughout one's lifetime (and beyond), is the ultimate cause of suffering. The mistake about the self leads to taking a "me," and what pertains to me, far too seriously, not realizing the ways in which the boundaries between persons are fortuitous and arbitrary. This in turn leads to desire. If a "me" is regarded as important, then it is all too easy to sink into egoism, urgently wanting things for myself. This, in Buddha's view, is the immediate cause of suffering.

Desire and Suffering

Hence, Buddha's practical advice, when he began to teach, was first and foremost that we lose our desires. This (like the Upanishads' recommendation to engross yourself in the identity of *atman* with Brahman) turns out to be very difficult, demanding dedication and full-time involvement in the work of changing one's habits of thought. Much of the practical arrangements of Buddhism as a movement came to center on this.

We need to understand why it was plausible to identify desire as the cause of suffering. Psychological insight is at work in the argument, but so too are niceties of language. The specific meanings that "desire" has had matter to the argument, as does the difference between pain and suffering.

It may be that the word "desire" is now in a process of broadening its most common meaning. Certainly many contemporary philosophers of psychology, who like to work with as simple and austere a set of key terms as they can manage, use the word "desire" generically for any want or preference. The dominant traditional use of "desire" is more narrow. You can desire something only if you don't have it but really would like to get it, or if you already have it and would hate to lose it. In addition you can desire things that are not intimately tied to yourself (e.g., world peace), but again only if they seem really important to you and if your feeling about not getting (or losing) them is strongly negative.

In short, to desire something (in the traditional meaning) is to have a strong appetite or preference for it, so strong that you would feel deeply disappointed if things did not turn out as you wished. To say, "If it's all the same, I'll take X instead of Y," when you would not much care if it simply turned out to be Y, is not to *desire* X. In much of life we have mild preferences, or faint and passing urges, that do not qualify as desires.

If the frustration of desires (in the traditional meaning) entails strong negative feelings, then presumably their satisfaction will involve significant positive feelings. There is a modern Western argument that links "desire" (in the narrow sense) with pleasure. This occurs in the fourth chapter of John Stuart Mill's *Utilitarianism*. Utilitarianism is an ethical theory that, in Mill's version, turns out to be a conjunction of two claims. One is consequentialism, the claim that the best thing to do is always determined by consequences, perhaps the likely consequences of the specific actions among which we must choose, or sometimes (as in the case of whether we should respect rights of free speech) the consequences of having one policy rather than another policy. The other claim is hedonism: that pleasure and only pleasure is good.

In his fourth chapter, Mill promises to give a "sort of proof" of his theory, although he then offers one only of the hedonism component. The argument is that desire has the same relation to what is desirable (i.e., good) as our physical senses have to physical reality, and that we desire pleasure and only pleasure. Hence the evidence is, Mill thinks, that pleasure and only pleasure is good.

How does Mill know that people desire pleasure and only pleasure? This is a sweeping claim, and on the face of it is empirical. Might there be people somewhere in the world who don't desire pleasure, or who desire something else? Perhaps research is needed?

Read closely, though, Mill appears to think that the argument does not rest on an empirical generalization. To desire something and to find it pleasant, he suggests, are fused in our thought: they are "phenomena entirely inseparable."

We may put to the side Mill's assumption that desire is *the* source of evidence of what has value. It is difficult to defend, and Buddha especially would have thought it both question begging and appalling. Here is a reconstruction of what the rest of Mill's argument might be. First of all, Mill makes clear that when he speaks of pleasure as the good, he means pleasure and the absence of pain. Desire hence is keyed to pleasure and the avoidance of pain. To desire X, as opposed to merely having a mild preference for it or thinking you might somewhat like it, is either (1) to think of X as pleasant, or (2) to find the thought of X pleasant (someone might in this way desire martyrdom while not thinking that the actual event will be pleasant), or (3) to think of not getting X as painful, or (4) to find the thought of not getting X painful. The link between desire and pleasure (and the avoidance of pain), if this part of the argument is correct, is logical rather than empirical.

You might ask yourself whether, if you prefer to have something but do not especially expect any pleasure in it, and if the thought of it is not particularly pleasant, and so on, would you label your feeling for it as "desire"? Given the traditional narrow sense of "desire," the answer surely has to be "No." This follows from the meanings of the available words.

Early Buddhist philosophers would agree with this analysis of desire. But they would follow it in a very different direction from Mill. They, like the writers of the Upanishads, hold not only that desire is a sick habit but also that a really good life requires that you give up pleasure. A Buddhist who does this can look forward to the bliss of nirvana, though, as a reward.

It is a short step from connecting desire and pleasure to connecting desire with suffering. The connection between desire and pleasure (and the avoidance of pain) is also a connection of thwarted desire with significant negative emotions. We can conjoin to this logical point the fact that, in everyone's real world, desire sometimes is thwarted.

The repeated Buddhist point is that to desire something goes beyond having a mild preference for it. It requires having an "attachment," in the sense that not getting (or losing) the thing would bring suffering. Because it is inevitable that we sometimes do not get or keep what we desire, it follows that if we have desires we will suffer.

The major elements of this argument are (1) an analysis of what is intrinsic to desire or craving, and (2) the factual claim that in the world of desiring no one always wins. This last connects of course with the realities of disease, old age, and death (which according to legend shocked Buddha). But it would be a mistake to limit human vulnerability to these areas. People who are used to desiring inevitably will want more money, popularity, importance, or love than they presently have; and if by good luck they get what they desire, this inevitably brings even more desire. Disease, old age, and death are (along with poverty) obvious sources of suffering. But people suffer also because those they care for go away, or because the arrangements of life are not what they would have liked, or because they are not connected with others in a satisfactory way. As Buddha saw it, there was a pandemic of suffering. He would think this even of the United States today, despite the relative prosperity and medical advances.

Hence desire makes suffering inevitable. The other side of this argument is that elimination of desire makes possible a life that will not include any suffering. In broad outline this may look right. But to appreciate what it really means, we need to get a full sense of what it might be like to have no desires. We also need to examine the concept of suffering.

Many people might think of pain and suffering as much the same or as inextricably linked. But—much as pleasure and happiness differ from one another, and joy and bliss differ still further—suffering is not exactly equivalent to misery, desolation, or distress, and certainly is separable from pain.

We speak of someone as suffering when she or he is in the grip of a negative emotional experience. Suffering can be rather brief. Someone can have terrible wounds, suffer intensely, but (mercifully) die within a few minutes. We normally speak of suffering, all the same, in cases in which, however long it actually will last, there is a sense of no end in sight. Could agony that predictably will last exactly two seconds count as suffering? We might not know what to say.

Suffering also typically involves passivity, a sense that the wound or the pain is in control and you simply must endure. Proven techniques of separating suffering from pain start from this insight. The childbirth techniques taught to expectant mothers are designed to enable women not to suffer while experiencing pain. They can escape suffering because their attention is caught up in processes of controlling what happens to them.

Similarly, Buddhists readily will admit that there is no way of entirely avoiding pain in life. After all, there are pain nerves in our bodies. But someone who can take control of her or his mental processes can experience pain without suffering. Alexandra David-Neel, who early in the twentieth century traveled through Buddhist Tibet disguised as a man, tells of a monk who was knifed by an attendant. The dying man, who was in great pain, cut short police questioning; he preferred not to be bothered by the pain and could avoid this by controlling his thoughts in meditation.

What is it to have met Buddha's standard for having lost all desires? Some readers may have the image of someone who is entirely listless, apathetic, and inert. But we need to bear in mind that a desire is an appetite or preference of a particularly intense and vulnerability-creating kind.

The account of Buddha after he had reached enlightenment (and presumably had lost all his desires) is instructive. He was not listless or inert. He clearly preferred to teach his technique of avoiding suffering. Did he *desire* to teach? Imaginably a crucial test would have been if someone had locked him up and prevented him from teaching. If that had made him severely disappointed or miserable, that would have been a bad sign: a sign that he still had desires. If, however, while still preferring to teach, he had not been terribly upset, that would have been a sign that he had lost his desires. It seems very likely that the latter would have been Buddha's response. The accounts give a picture of someone who has a steady purpose (and in this sense is not apathetic) but who was not wound up in it and was prepared to be detached and to take what came.

Loss of Desire, and the Natures of Love and Altruism

The most common misunderstanding of Buddha's recommendations occurs especially among students who have been brought up to be very nice people. Often they assume that Buddha is urging us to lose our selfish desires. This seems to them clearly to make sense, in that a world without selfishness might be assumed to be more peaceful and happy.

But Buddha urges us to lose all of our desires, selfish and unselfish ones alike. This is built into the logic of the argument. To desire is to be vulnerable to suffering, period. Even if, somehow, we limit our desires to those for the well-being of others, to have something as strong as a desire exposes us to the contingencies of life. What happens when, say, the people we care so much about are defeated or die? We will suffer.

Someone who understands this may come to think that, even if Buddha's arguments are entirely valid, the cure (to the problem of suffering) that he proposes may be worse than the disease. This is of course a matter for individual judgment. But we can get a clearer picture of what the stakes are if we explore the dimensions of the kind of life Buddha is recommending.

What would it be like to have lost all your desires? The most obvious point is that you would appear a cool and detached person, never upset or really worried. Would you seem blank and affectless? The answer depends in part on whether one thinks there is something characteristically human and positive that will remain, and become more noticeable, once desires have vanished. Some later schools of Buddhist philosophy developed the idea that everyone has a "Buddha nature," which would be evident once desires were eliminated.

If there is a "Buddha nature," it is not like an *atman*. There is no suggestion that we are all one spiritual reality. The "Buddha nature" is not characterless. Rather the idea seems to be that our desire-laden lives inevitably are dominated by concerns for self. These preoccupy us. Once this layer of concern and anxiety is removed, we will not feel neutral; rather, we will feel good. Our minds will be far less cluttered and more open to other people and to life. There will be a low-intensity (but steady) positive affect such as that exhibited by the Buddha after he reached enlightenment.

This transformation in you would be in a way a transformation in your orientation toward time. Desires are always or almost always for something in the future. If we strongly prefer that the past were different, this is a wish and not a desire. To live in desires is constantly to be looking forward. Some writers have noted a common human tendency to think that one's life, right now, is not really as it should be; but next week (or when I get the promotion, or when I get married, or when . . .) it will be settled properly. Typically the magic moment when life is as it should be never comes. This makes human existence rather like the inner life of greyhounds chasing wooden rabbits around a track.

Part of what gets lost is the present. We may lose joy; we certainly lose the detail of what is before us, and much of the wonder of it. One of the later schools of Buddhism, Zen (which will be discussed in chapter 8), particularly emphasizes this. A persistent idea in the Zen literature is that the world, on a minute-to-minute basis, is beautiful, but that we lose the beauty (and fail to take in most of the detail) because of our desire-laden thrust into the future.

What of love? Many would insist that the word "love" covers a variety of states, some more desire-laden than others. In the literature of Christianity there is a basic distinction between eros and agape. Agape is positive fellow feeling for other human beings and can be thought of as having the warmth of friendship or of good community relations.

It might seem obvious that someone who eliminates desires would have to give up on eros but could maintain agape. This, however, may be too simple on both counts. It is true that erotic love typically involves desires, not only for the well-being of the beloved but also for a close relationship. Can there be desireless eros? This might seem like a contradiction in terms, and it is true that Buddha stipulated that people who were serious about losing all of their desires should give up sexual relations (and family life) and become nuns or monks. But some later Tantric schools of Buddhism experimented with the possibility of highly detached eros, and it is not clear that desireless eros really is self-contradictory.

Agape, on the other hand, often is desire-laden. We can care deeply for our friends and members of our community, and can suffer when bad things happen to them. Our concern for our children and our parents can be especially intense.

Buddha believes that someone who is really serious about enlightenment will give up this intensity of concern. His recommendations with regard to lessening attachment though are tempered by the realization that the great majority of his followers will be unwilling (and perhaps unable) to transform their lives in the extreme way that this would require. Hence Buddhist ethics in effect specifies two tracks in life. The recommendations for someone who wanted merely to have a good life, without striving for final enlightenment, were in large part that she or he follow a morality on the whole similar to those that are familiar in most civilized societies. There were some additions, the major one being that all taking of life (including animal life) is forbidden. Animals, as chapter 10 of the Dhammapada points out, do not want to die, and tend to suffer if threatened or killed. Buddha held that we should all be considerate of that.

Besides this track, which allowed for family life, there was a more demanding path for those who sought enlightenment. They should become nuns or monks and give up *all* strong concern for any individuals. One simply should not be affectively close to anyone. There is a long poem, "The Rhinoceros," included in Conze's *Buddhist Scriptures*, that expresses this. The refrain is "Fare lonely as rhinoceros."

Someone who has lost her or his desires can be expected to exhibit a gentle warmth toward everyone. Special warmth, though, risks suffering if things go wrong.

This warmth is connected with Buddhist altruism, which (despite the extreme opposition between Buddha's and John Stuart Mill's views of desire) is like the altruism advocated by some contemporary utilitarians. The word "altruism" has a range of meanings. It can refer in general to practical caring for other people, to not being entirely selfish. A strong form of altruism is that of taking everyone's interests as equally important, counting oneself merely as one person. In this strong form of altruism, one would not favor oneself, or one's family or friends, or one's community over the interests of strangers.

Some readers may think that this is not humanly possible, or that if it is possible it is inhuman. Some philosophers (including some utilitarians) share this reaction to the point at which they would circumscribe the ideal, relying on a distinction between a sphere of private life and one of social policy. In private life, they suggest, it is desirable to favor

family, friends, and community (and also oneself), at least to a modest degree. But social policy, they urge, should be disinterested—in the traditional meaning in which to be disinterested is to be impartial.

One difficulty with this approach is in knowing how to draw the line between what should be regarded as private, on one hand, and, on the other hand, cases in which the pressing needs of strangers should transform the way in which we make our decisions. In any event Buddha's altruism is not partitioned in the manner just described.

Let me conclude this section by summarizing some of the major misgivings that many readers might have about Buddha's solution to the problem of suffering, and also what the likely replies of an early Buddhist philosopher might have been. Some might think that the most highly recommended kind of life lacks excitement. A likely reply would have been that one should not see the alternatives as excitement or boredom. A serious follower of Buddha does give up what most people would regard as excitement, but there is a promise (which we will explore shortly) of a resultant joy or bliss.

Secondly, many might think that to pursue enlightenment is to give up on love. The likely reply is "Yes and no." Certainly the intense forms of love that preoccupy most of us, whether erotic or love for family and friends, would disappear. But the follower of Buddha might argue that these attachment-laden forms of love, besides creating vulnerability to suffering, also often create problems for those who are loved and those who love. People become preoccupied with attractions or loyalties, or hurts and disappointments, and because of this fail to settle harmoniously into the rhythms of life. The low-intensity universal love that remains available to the serious Buddhist, it might be argued, is easier (and in the long run more satisfying) to live with.

Finally, it might be objected that the ideal of Buddhist altruism, its rejection of selfishness and its denial that particular ties should have any special power over us, simply goes against human nature. A reply might be that the human nature that we are born with is a rough beginning, one that is liable to difficulties and contradictions. It is wise to develop a nature that goes well beyond this and that irons out the contradictions.

This kind of answer is not as unique to early Buddhist philosophy as one might suppose. The Upanishads also question first-stage human nature, which they argue puts us in the grip of illusion. The Confucian philosopher Xunzi (Hsun-Tzu), who lived in the third century BCE, argued that first-stage human nature is inherently defective and needs to be bent into a different shape if we are to have

The Greek philosopher Aristotle also can be argued to hold that a really good life requires the achievement of a second nature, which represents the shaping of first-stage nature—initially by youthful habits reinforced by the influence of pleasure and pain, and secondly by philosophical understanding.

The Path to Enlightenment

Buddha certainly regarded first-stage human nature as creating problems. Chapter 3 of the Dhammapada begins "The mind is wavering and restless, difficult to guard and restrain: let the wise man straighten his mind as the maker of arrows makes his arrows straight" (Mascaro translation, p. 40). Chapter 1 includes the recommendation of extreme watchfulness over the mind, so that passions do not break in (as they are prone to do). Chapter 24 begins with the warning that if someone does not focus on nirvana, which is the final state of enlightenment, then that person is vulnerable to cravings, which "grow like a creeper" (Mascaro translation, p. 83).

Much of the regimen, then, for those seriously pursuing enlightenment, will consist of techniques for steadying and controlling the mind. In a way morality is an essential part of this. Immorality, above and beyond the obvious negative things that can be said about it, is disruptive. Typically it involves desires. In most civilized societies, after all, following the established moral code is simply the path of least resistance (except perhaps for those in dire want). In this way immorality is a bad sign in relation to enlightenment: it typically signals the presence of ungoverned desires. Typically also immorality sets up sources of anxiety, and the likelihood of conflicts with others. All in all, it would disable any pursuit of enlightenment.

Immorality thus goes deeply against self-interest. For a serious follower of Buddha who is still at an early enough stage that self-interest retains a hold, this is yet one more reason against immorality. For someone who has progressed far enough that self-interest no longer has psychological weight, immorality (with its array of desires and conflicts) simply will be psychologically impossible.

The search for enlightenment, then, will subsume morality, as a matter of course. It also will involve other habits of life conducive to calmness and steadiness. Meditation, like that associated with the classic Hindu view of the Upanishads, will be devoted to engrossing the mind in the vision of the world thought most definitively true. In the

case of the Upanishads, this had to emphasize boundary-dissolving, so that the world could be seen entirely as one cosmic unity. Buddha's metaphysics is not one of cosmic unity, so that the nature and goals of meditation become different. Meditation serves to focus more sharply the nature of the problem of suffering, and the fortuitousness of the boundaries among the selves among whom suffering is distributed. In some Buddhist traditions there is a preference for meditation in grave-yards, or in places where skulls are to be found, as a way of concen-trating the mind on the most basic facts of human life.

The end result of the loss of the importance given to a distinct self, and the loss of desires, is a mind with no consuming cravings, worries, or anxieties. It is a mind from which much that gives "nor-mal" human life its character has been cleared. This is held to leave room for joy. The Dhammapada speaks of the "joy of silence." Nir-vana, which is the ultimate reward of enlightenment, involves joy or bliss as a feature of a state (which persists after death) that is indescrib-able. It is indescribable because it is so different from anything that people normally experience, so that linguistic categories are not avail-able to describe it. In chapter 2 of the Dhammapada (Mascaro transla-tion) it is spoken of as "the peace supreme and infinite joy."

Conclusion

It needs to be emphasized that many readers who know something about Buddhism, including some who are practicing Buddhists, may find the account of early Buddhist philosophy in this chapter different from what they are familiar with. There are now a wide variety of forms of Buddhism in the world, each of them retaining points of contact with the earliest texts but very different from some of the others. This historical diversification is hardly unique to Buddhism. (Was Jesus a Southern Baptist?) It can be argued that virtually every late form does capture something important that is present in, or at least hinted at, in early texts. Complicated issues arise from the fact, however, that some of these forms include accounts of what Buddha *really* taught, in some cases portraying him as having an inner core of teaching that was not accessible to most of his disciples (who got the simple version) and hence was not represented in early texts. This chapter does not take sides on these issues: what I mean by early Bud-dhism is simply the Buddhist philosophy that is represented in early texts, such as the Dhammapada.

The Dhammapada centers on the problem of suffering. There is a diagnosis of the causes of suffering, which include an incorrect metaphysics that takes the separate self too seriously, treating a fortuitous bundle of thoughts and experiences as if it were a substance. More immediately, desire and addiction to pleasure cause suffering. The solution is to see through the separate self, give up pleasures, and to lose all one's desires (both the selfish and the unselfish ones).

To do this is not easy. It requires sustained effort and undivided attention. In practice only nuns and monks have any chance of success. Even ordinary people are expected by the Buddha to follow a morality somewhat more demanding than the one most of us are used to. This morality includes the prohibition of any taking of life, human or animal. Humans and animals alike tend to want not to die, and are likely to suffer if they are killed or feel threatened with death. Really serious followers of Buddha can conquer this vulnerability to suffering by losing their desires and cultivating a degree of detachment, but most humans (and all animals) cannot.

The ultimate solution to the problem of suffering would be for all beings ultimately to liberate themselves from false metaphysics and from desires. This would be an extraordinarily prolonged process, which would include the reincarnation of animals as humans and—very likely over many lifetimes—the attainment of enlightenment. The interim solution requires compassion for those who are not able to free themselves from vulnerability to suffering. Those who can liberate themselves should be encouraged to do so. The Buddha provides only what amounts to a do-it-yourself kit for liberation, so that in the last analysis enlightenment is a matter of individual effort. The rewards, though, are great, including freedom from anxiety and finally nirvana, an eternity of joy.

Recommended Reading

The Questions of King Milinda, trans. T. W. Rhys Davids, was first published as volumes 35 and 36 (1890, 1894) of the Oxford *Sacred Books of the East,* and was reprinted by Dover Books (1963). It presents a systematic account, with considerable explicit argument, of early Buddhist philosophy.

Edward Conze, *Buddhism: Its Essence and Development* (Oxford: Bruno Cassirer, 1951) provides an extremely readable general account of Buddhism.

Edward Conze, *Buddhist Scriptures* (Harmondsworth: Penguin, 1959) is a very usable collection.

Steven Collins, *Selfless Persons* (Cambridge: Cambridge University Press, 1982) offers a careful analysis of the Buddhist denial of self.

Thomas P. Kasulis, "The Buddhist Concept of Self," in *A Companion to World Philosophies,* ed. Eliot Deutsch and Ron Bontekoe (Oxford: Blackwell, 1997), pp. 400–409, is clear and good on the same subject.

T. R. V. Murti, *The Central Philosophy of Buddhism* (London: George Allen & Unwin, 1955) provides a philosophically sophisticated and readable analysis of the later development of a major school of Buddhist philosophy, Madhyamika.

Jay Garfield's translation of, and commentary on, the great Madhyamika philosopher Nagarjuna (*The Fundamental Wisdom of the Middle Way* [New York: Oxford University Press, 1995]) is useful and an impressive achievement.

THREE

THE BHAGAVAD GITA

Buddhism and Buddhist philosophy had a great impact on India, becoming strongly competitive with Hinduism and the philosophy of the Upanishads, and eventually (but only for a while) gaining the upper hand. Hinduism, though, had considerable vitality left in it. Plainly part of the appeal of Buddhism, especially close to the grassroots level, was that it offered possibilities of life, including a feeling of connectedness with others, that seemed richer to many than the austere withdrawal mandated for those who really took seriously the ethics of the Upanishads. The Bhagavad Gita presents a philosophy of Hinduism that in a way meets this Buddhist challenge, by also offering greater possibilities, including the possible combination of spiritual enlightenment with active participation in the world.

The philosophy of the Bhagavad Gita at the deepest level agrees with that of the Upanishads. It remains the case that *atman* is Brahman. It also remains the case that liberation can be achieved by an austere and difficult full realization of this. However, the Bhagavad Gita goes beyond these claims, offering a rich menu of options for arriving at a life consonant with the identity of *atman* and Brahman. In the new dispensation, there are multiple forms of the ethical ideal instead of a single ideal. In the process, the Bhagavad Gita presents a subtle psychology of action and of love, and a dramatic vision of how someone can be in the world and yet not really in it.

The Dilemma

The Bhagavad Gita takes place in the middle of a very long story. The full narrative is the *Mahabharata*, an ancient Indian epic (that scholars now think dates from about 100 BCE) that in some ways corresponds to Homer's *Iliad*. The epic recounts a struggle for kingship between two branches of the same family. The hero of the story is Arjuna, a gifted and sensitive warrior. To say that Arjuna is a warrior is not merely to describe what he does. It is also to place him in Indian society: in the noble warrior caste, which (along with the Brahmin, priestly caste) was at the top of the caste system.

The other main character in the Bhagavad Gita is the god Krishna. We have already seen, in relation to the Upanishads, that classical Hindu metaphysics is one of multiple identities. In the superficial framework of reality in which virtually all of us actually live, your identity is as an individual with characteristics unlikely to be even nearly duplicated by anyone else. In ancient India your caste status would have been an important part of this individual identity. At the same time, in the framework of ultimate reality, you are an *atman* that is Brahman, like one drop of water in a spiritual ocean.

Krishna's identity is especially complex. Folk Hinduism had developed the idea that high gods could have a series of births as gods. In effect the high god could take many forms. Krishna is a bodily incarnation (an avatar) of the god Vishnu. At the same time, like all of the gods and goddesses, and like us, he is (in the framework of ultimate reality) really Brahman. The difference here between the part or aspect of Brahman that is Krishna and the part or aspect that is you or me is that Krishna is really aware of his Brahman nature and can manipulate his presentation to reflect this.

Nevertheless, the Krishna of folk Hinduism is normally portrayed as a handsome, exceptionally amorous young man, always wooing women although there is one special favorite, Radha. In the Indian miniature paintings that are to be found in the great museums of the world, Krishna is a frequent subject and is easily recognizable. He is blue.

The Krishna of the Bhagavad Gita is driving the chariot of the warrior-hero Arjuna. It is on the eve of what promises to be a great battle. Two armies are ready to engage. Arjuna seems confident of victory but all the same is troubled. He foresees that in the battle he will kill members of his own extended family who are fighting on the other side. He is very reluctant to do this, and one way to avoid it would be to refuse to fight. Fortunately, there is someone he can ask for advice, his charioteer, the god Krishna.

The Bhagavad Gita is Krishna's reply. It is a relatively small part of the long *Mahabharata,* but is long enough to be a book in its own right. What Krishna says ranges outward from the specific dilemma to the general problems of life, including ruminations on the nature of the universe. Altogether it amounts to a complete philosophy, including both metaphysics and ethics. This philosophy adroitly manages to be very different from that of the Upanishads, without contradicting it at any point.

In exploring this philosophy, we need to be mindful of some distinctions. One is within ethics. Much of ethics is concerned with how we should behave. When the issue is how we should behave in matters of real urgency, in which a wrong choice might be viewed as warranting deep regret on the agent's part and severe censure on the part of the rest of us, we tend to classify it as one of morality. If the issue is of lesser urgency, and wrong choices are viewed as exhibiting foolishness or tastelessness, we tend to classify it as one of ordinary practical life or perhaps of etiquette. Finally, there are issues that are not primarily ones of how we should behave, but rather of what it is best to aim for (or to avoid) in life. These are issues of what has value (in a narrow sense of "value"), and are sometimes placed under the heading of axiology.

The ethics of the Bhagavad Gita begins from morality: specifically the moral issue of whether it is right for Arjuna to fight and to kill his relatives. It then broadens out to consideration of the kind of life that would be most fulfilling for Arjuna, or for that matter for anyone. The issues here are not what we would normally think of as moral but rather ones of value (axiology). Discussion of what the most desirable kinds of life are is closely linked to the world picture, the metaphysics, of the Bhagavad Gita.

The Morality of the Bhagavad Gita

Questions of the morality of certain kinds of actions in general hinge on what the actions really amount to. Just what are you doing if you do that? In a narrow view, this question will focus on what is immediately involved in what someone does.

Much may depend on whether we treat consequences as part of what is done, or as separate (even though they may have been predictable). Bloggs says that he merely has moved his finger against the trigger of a gun. He might want to describe it that way, but really he has shot someone. That is, we can insist that the immediate consequence of an action (the consequence of Bloggs moving his finger) counts as part of what is being done. Whether more remote consequences count as part of what is being done, or count in a different way as separate from the deed itself, might be debated as part of the question of how the act is to be described. If the consequences are foreseeable and able to be taken for granted, we might regard them as part of the act itself.

Bearing this in mind, we can ask just what Arjuna will be doing if he kills his relatives. In our ordinary way of looking at things, this is first and foremost his bringing about loss of life. Thus, part of killing someone is a minus—at least for the person killed. In a culture that takes reincarnation entirely for granted, though, there will have to be a different ordinary way of looking at things. Generally speaking, Krishna reminds Arjuna, to die is to enter a new life. The relatives that Arjuna is about to kill will live again. Therefore to kill them is not, in fact, to deprive them of life. How, then, can it involve harming them?

There is beneath this another layer of argument. In the framework of ultimate reality, we all are Brahman. Brahman remains Brahman. Whatever we think we are doing, really it changes nothing. Hence Arjuna's worry about killing his relatives is misplaced. Nothing he will do will make any real difference to anything.

This metaphysical reflection might seem to lead to an ethics of profound indifference, although in fact it does not. Within the framework of superficial reality, which is where the writer and the readers of the Bhagavad Gita actually spend their waking lives, much of what we do does make a significant difference. Nevertheless, the first of Krishna's two arguments (the one about reincarnation) is keyed to this framework and remains troubling. The claim that killing really does no harm, because those killed are reincarnated, might seem to suggest that anyone can feel free to kill anyone else, at any moment. (It is no big deal.) If we take seriously the second argument (that, because Brahman remains Brahman, whatever one does really amounts to nothing), this would suggest that all actions are equally justified or equally unjustified.

If these were its conclusions, the Bhagavad Gita would not have a morality. Downplaying the ordinary, instinctive sense that killing someone makes a significant difference to the world is, however, only a first step in the moral argument of the book. It clears the ground for what will determine moral judgment in the absence of serious consequences.

This is caste status. If killing makes no major difference in the superficial swirl of death and rebirth, and amounts to nothing at all in the ultimate reality of Brahman, then the social responsibilities of caste serve as a moral default position. Krishna reminds Arjuna that he is in the warrior caste, and his required function—in situations like the present one—is to fight and kill his opponents.

Many Western readers will find this pattern of argument jarring. Our culture is used to the idea of a universalistic ethics, which like the law applies irrespective of persons (or of the different social statuses of various persons). Formally, of course, Krishna's advice is universalistic: it is that everyone should behave along the lines of her or his caste obligations. But the detailed recommendations that this entails will vary, obviously, with the caste of the person who is applying the universal recommendation. In this respect, the implication of the Bhagavad Gita is that not everyone should be governed by the same morality.

The contrast between this and modern Western moralities may be less sharp than one at first supposes. First, Western moralities typically take account of obligations that grow out of particular relationships, such as marriage, friendship, or the parent-child link. A morality can include a universal recommendation that anyone who is a parent has special responsibilities for his or her children. It has been debated in recent years whether the most influential modern Western ethical theories can do full justice to the claims of special relationships, especially if the theories insist on viewing the obligations that they generate as making the same kind of claim as that involved in the obligation to keep promises or to treat other people justly. It has been suggested by the psychologist Carol Gilligan, in her *In a Different Voice,* that many women give moral weight to particular relationships in a way in which few men do.

Whatever one thinks of these debates, the obvious point is that they concern how personal relationships can be taken account of in ethics. Krishna's moral advice to Arjuna centers not on personal relationships, but rather on the warrior's caste status. Plainly this will be a morality that will have its locus in a deferential society, in which someone's position in the social hierarchy is held to generate duties of a specific sort, appropriate to that position. Such a deferential society is not that far in the past in the West, as the title of a well-regarded nineteenth-century book for women who were becoming servants, *My Station and Its Duties,* attests.

Losing One's Self

The Upanishads had relatively little to say about morality, concentrating instead on the truths that necessitated a life of spiritual concentration, as well as the regimen that it would require. That the Bhagavad Gita gives more prominent attention to morality is of course a function of its placement within a long dramatic narrative. But it also is part of the work's concern with real life as most people live it, and with its attempt to reach a wide audience with varying concerns. Nevertheless, the Bhagavad Gita, like the Upanishads, in the end is most concerned with nonmoral issues of how one leads a deeply gratifying life of the highest quality.

Why aren't these moral issues? Part of the answer is that there is nothing immoral about leading a humdrum and unsatisfying life. Quality of life issues—which are what the Bhagavad Gita pays most attention to—are not the same as issues that center on possible harm to others (which are at the core of morality) or on violations of societal taboos (which many would include in the subject matter of morality).

Here is a short version of what the Bhagavad Gita recommends. It is loss of self. This capsule summary, though, has to be prelude to a much longer account. We need to understand what counts as loss of self. What is this self that is lost? Why would loss of self contribute so greatly to quality of life? And what are the varieties of loss of self?

There are two Sanskrit terms, *atman* and *jiva,* that might with some plausibility be translated as "self." *Atman,* as we have seen in our discussion of the Upanishads, is claimed to be the core reality of anyone, the inner nature minus anything that is individual and changeable. *Atman* thus is the most minimalist kind of self. It is Brahman, and clearly there is no way in which it can be lost.

Jiva is the individual self. Each of us has a *jiva,* but there is a sense in which *jiva* can be lost. The process of fully realizing your oneness with Brahman is, viewed in the framework of superficial reality, a process of transformation in which you become increasingly impersonal and lose individual features.

The various ideals presented in the Bhagavad Gita have some resemblance to this withering away of *jiva.* The text repeatedly emphasizes that the ideals require the insight, into one's true relation to Brahman, that is conveyed in the Upanishads. Nevertheless, I think that merely to equate the recommendations of the Bhagavad Gita with the loss of *jiva* would be too simple and neat. Indeed, the Bhagavad Gita could be interpreted as offering spiritual possibilities in which a somewhat purified *jiva* plays a role.

Instead, a helpful approach can start from the occasions of everyday life in which we might speak of someone as losing her or his self. The most crude and obvious cases are those in which we speak of someone as, say, losing herself in her work. Most cases of this sort are loss of self only to a limited degree, in that we are willing to speak of "losing oneself" even when there is some intermittent awareness of the general character of one's life and of the prospects for success of the work. "Losing oneself," then, is a way of speaking of a *degree* of distraction from the general character of one's life and projects.

Total absorption would be a clearer case of loss of self in this colloquial sense. Skilled sequential activities sometimes come close to total absorption, as someone becomes carried along with the activity and is at the same time abstracted from the character of her or his individual life. The psychologist Mihalyi Csikszentmihalyi, in his *Flow: The Psychology of Optimal Experience,* has presented evidence for regarding such experiences as the most deeply gratifying in life.

A case could be made for holding that experiences of sexual ecstasy also take people out of themselves. This may be one reason that the exteriors of some Hindu temples, such as the famous one at Khajuraho, are decorated with highly erotic sculptures. It is not that the eroticism is part of the religion; rather, it represents the most vivid experience that some worshipers will have had of loss of self, and in this respect is a sort of introduction to the goals of the religion. The introduction, though, falls far short of the final goals. The erotic loss of self is of limited duration, and there may well be a "rebound" factor. The Bhagavad Gita must be seen as pursuing ideals of loss of self that is ongoing, rather than being a matter of experiences now and then.

The colloquial sense of "loss of self" that I have been exploring really amounts to loss of sense of self. *Atman* is never lost. *Jiva*, I think, would have to wither away in a life in which someone gets "outside of" her or his self for increasing periods of time. But this may not be entirely clear, and I think it helpful to concentrate in this discussion on the possibilities for ongoing loss of sense of self.

One aspect should be noted of such phenomena as losing oneself in the flow of skilled activity or losing oneself in a moment of ecstasy. The sense of time becomes different from what it normally is, or perhaps it would be more accurate to say that there is no longer any sense of time. Perhaps the feeling, in relation to time sense, is indescribable. But clearly one mark of a different relation to time is that the absorbed person does not have specific thoughts about the future, such as about how things will turn out. To think "What will I have for breakfast tomorrow?" is not truly to be in ecstasy, or to be truly absorbed in a creative project. The skilled worker who has thoughts about the prizes that might be won is, also, not entirely absorbed in the project.

Someone who entered this line of thought from a background in ancient folk Hinduism might naturally relate the loss of self to one activity traditionally of great importance, that of sacrificing to the gods. Such sacrifices were important in many ancient religions. The sacrifices reported in the Old Testament, with the significant exception of Jephthah's daughter (Judges 11. 12), are of animals. Many ancient Near-Eastern peoples engaged in sacrifice of firstborn children, and among the many meanings that scholars have sometimes claimed to find in the biblical story of Abraham and Isaac (in which God commands Abraham to sacrifice his son Isaac but at the last minute substitutes a ram) is that it might function as a "just so" story about a transition from human to animal sacrifice.

Much of the motivation for sacrifices had to be linked to the hope that the gods (or God) would reward the worshiper who proved his devotion by sacrificing. This easily could amount to a crude attempt to make a contract with divinities, along the lines of "Here is something for you, and please reciprocate by giving me a good harvest (or by healing the sick in my family)." If all of this seems alien to the modern reader, reflect that sometimes the psychology of prayer is not altogether different. People sometimes pray altruistically (e.g., for world peace), but it may be that the most highly motivated prayers are by and large for personal rewards or protection.

A subtle mind might be uneasy about this self-oriented nature of religious activity. The story of Nachiketas in the Katha Upanishad (discussed in chapter 1) illustrates such a response. The thought is that a religious person first and foremost should abandon herself or himself before the divine, rather than attempting to buy or beg favor. If religious activity (as it traditionally did at the time of the Bhagavad Gita) involves sacrifices, these sacrifices should be expressions of devotion, which will be pure only if they include no thoughts of reward.

Here are two observations about this line of thought. One is that it leads in the same direction as the remarks earlier about the changed experience of time implicit in loss of self. The devoted, unselfish person who offers sacrifices with no thought of reward has, in effect, blocked the most obvious thoughts about the future (such as "What will this get me?") that might normally occur at such moments. This is a large step toward closing off thoughts of the future and instead being absorbed in the devotion of the moment.

Second, to sacrifice without thoughts of reward does not entail that there will be no chance of some kind of reward. Here are two sets of experiences from ordinary (nonreligious) life that may shed light on what is involved here. Imagine first someone who gives you a present, at the same time saying "What will you now give me?" If this kind of "generosity" seems unappealing, then think of the position of a Hindu god or goddess who is a target of a sacrifice accompanied by prayer. (In the Katha Upanishad the position is made more extreme by the fact that the cattle sacrificed are described as not being of high quality. Think of getting a present you didn't even want from someone who wants something in return.)

In fact, most of us do reciprocate presents and favors when we can. This reciprocal behavior adds to the texture of friendship and love, but only in the absence of explicit expectation of reciprocation. Even a sense of tacit calculation on the part of a giver would spoil everything.

The other phenomenon of everyday life that is worth keeping in mind is this. Some major values in life are reached best by not taking direct or conscious aim at them. Happiness is the best known example. It has become a cliché that self-conscious pursuits of happiness, with frequent calculation of what will lead to the most happiness, often are self-defeating. An unself-conscious coherence in life and in the pursuit of projects can be more effective.

Similarly, when the Bhagavad Gita urges the reader to sacrifice to the gods without thought of reward, this need not imply a diminished probability of there eventually being some reward. As we will see, in fact the Bhagavad Gita holds that there will be great rewards in the paths of life that it recommends. But, like many rewards in life, these benefits may not be what the giving person originally had in mind.

Options

The Upanishads had outlined one clear route to loss of sense of self. An initial step is acknowledging that your *atman* is Brahman. The further steps that lead to this vision's coming to engross your thinking are more difficult. They require meditation, techniques of concentration (i.e., yoga), and the elimination of sources of distraction. This much is evident in the Upanishads. It is plausible to suppose that there came to be considerable experience, during the centuries after the philosophy of the Upanishads became established, of what worked and what didn't work.

What, then, was the life like of someone aiming for the deepest loss of self? The story of the mystics with whom Buddha consorted, in the initial phase of his quest for enlightenment, suggests that food deprivation could be viewed as important. The obvious thought is that food energy fuels distracting thoughts, some of which moreover may be of a lustful nature. This line of thought has had a long history: witness Tolstoy's story *The Kreutzer Sonata*, which moves effortlessly from a condemnation of sexual license to a harangue against excessive meat eating on the part of the Russian privileged classes.

Attempting to get things done also clearly carries risks. First of all, the activity may grow out of desire; and desires lead to further desires as well as to other disturbing emotions, such as frustration. Even the desire to become engrossed in the vision of *atman* as Brahman, and to gain salvation, is suspect. It is useful at the start; but, when other desires are lost, it too must be lost.

Even activities that are not grounded in desire, and that instead are entered into in a spirit of "Might as well," have risks. There may be difficulties and complications, and one risk is that there will be distracting thoughts of "Will this succeed?" Hence the traditional view came to be that reaching the ideal of the Upanishads required passivity and inaction, rather than action. One simply sat and meditated and *did* as little as possible.

Krishna argues that this is fallacious. Any time one has a choice, the null option (i.e., not doing whatever it is) represents a choice so that one *is* doing something. Being passive and still was something that Buddha's companions *did*. If we accept this point, then we have to agree that, in a way, to be alive is to engage in action, even if the action may be of the still, quiet kind.

This line of thinking suggests two further thoughts. If action, of some kind, is inevitable, then perhaps what matters is not whether we eliminate action (which Krishna argues is, strictly speaking, impossible) but rather the attitude with which we do whatever we do. The second thought is that, if attitude is the key to enlightenment and liberation, then there is no obvious reason that someone who is in fact highly active (like the warrior Arjuna) could not have the right kind of attitude.

This argument is accompanied by a scrupulous insistence that the path of life recommended by the Upanishads can work. It certainly will succeed for an extremely committed person of the right kind. However, many will find all of the sitting and immobility frustrating, and in the end not at all conducive to calm. Someone like the energetic Arjuna, for example, will have great difficulty in not becoming restless if he embarks on a regimen of semistarvation and quiet meditation.

Sacrifices to a god or goddess would go under the heading of "works," as the term is sometimes used for meritorious religious activities. (The original debate between Martin Luther and the Roman Catholic Church was in large part over whether the Church was right in holding that works, as well as faith, counted directly toward salvation.) More broadly of course, sacrificing is an activity. It may be natural, then, to move from the thought that sacrifices should be performed without thought of reward to the much larger claim that in general activities should be performed without thought of reward, or indeed without thought of the future. To live consistently like this would be a kind of loss of self.

It also would be, to borrow a phrase from a different tradition, to be like the lilies of the field. Presumably the ideal is not meant to encourage carelessness or any euphoric taking of unnecessary risks. One may well have some sense of the possible (or likely) shape of the future, but one does not *think* about it in any sense that implies concern or fixation on winning, losing, reward, or punishment. Instead there is absorption in the activity itself, so that the actor becomes—for that period of time—the movements and rhythms of what is done.

Someone of an active and energetic temperament, like Arjuna, will find this ideal far more congenial than the austere and passive behavior that had evolved from the Upanishads. There would be some convergence of viewpoints between the two ideals: the central idea remains that *atman* is Brahman. But the styles of life, especially on the surface, would be very different. To engross oneself in the knowledge of one's true identity as Brahman, through disciplined quiet meditation, requires surrendering a great deal of normal everyday life. Family life, with its distractions and risks of disturbance, has to be abandoned. So does any kind of career, business, or other form of active engagement with other people and with the world.

Someone who aims to lose himself or herself in activity, on the other hand, need not abandon a career, business, or other form of active engagement with other people and with the world. What is required is an overriding detachment, so that one will never worry about any form of failure or desire success. If we assume that this detachment does not preclude awareness of the likely shape of the future, it might actually improve performance. The result would be much like what athletes speak of as entering "the zone." There are comparable phenomena in relation to other kinds of performance. People are usually at their best when they become entirely absorbed in what they are doing and are not distracted by concerns about outcomes.

It should be added that someone whose vitality is not frittered away on a multitude of small and large concerns will have much more energy where it counts. Being focused is really energizing. In this way, the Bhagavad Gita, which encourages lack of concern for success, paradoxically can be thought of as a manual for how to gain greater energy, of the sort that leads to success.

Someone who aims to lose herself or himself in activity also can have involvements, including a family life, that on the surface look normal. Indeed such relationships can be, by some standards, highly successful. It could be argued, for example, that relationships (such as those between parents and children) sometimes are impaired by one or more of the parties caring too much about outcomes.

Nevertheless, clearly the "love" that a highly detached person can have might well lack something from the point of view of those who are loved. Does true love require concern for the future and the vulnerability that goes along with that? Many people would answer "Yes." Nevertheless, highly detached people imaginably could continue all or almost all of the patterns implicit in normal relations, and life with them would be highly likely not to be tense.

A natural question is whether love itself, including the familiar forms of romantic love, can serve as a vehicle for loss of self. Can we consider love, of a certain sort, a viable option, along with action and meditative contemplation, as a way of losing oneself (and having the *jiva* wither away)? Denis de Rougemont, in *Love in the Western World,* argued that there is an inner connection between the Western tradition of incandescent erotic love, on one hand, and death, on the other. It is hardly an accident, in his view, that Tristan and Isolde ended up as they did. It is not at all clear, though, whether the love he considers involves loss of self or instead represents expanded claims of self beyond reason. Further his account leaves room for other forms of love, including agape and successful married love, which he clearly regards as different from the self-destructiveness of ideal Western eros.

The possible connections between love and loss of self may be more complicated than one might first suppose. Let us start with the forms of love, including romantic love, that are most familiar to us. It is clear that both strongly felt romantic love and love such as that of a parent for a child can involve an experience of loss of self. The normal forms, in both cases, involve two sorts of concern, which conceivably could diverge. On one hand, the person who loves wishes the well-being and happiness of the one loved. We would hardly consider the emotion love if this concern were absent. (The emotion might then seem more like a predatory desire to appropriate.) On the other hand, the person who loves typically wishes for a future close connection between the loved one and herself or himself. This close connection is to include reciprocation of the love.

Plainly love of this sort is a mixed emotion, with elements both of selflessness (desire for the well-being of the other) and selfishness (desire for reciprocation of the love). Occasionally these two elements pull in drastically different directions. For example, it may become evident that the well-being of the loved one can be assured only at the cost of future connection with the one who loves. The literature of romance has dwelt on the poignant cases in which this conflict has led to a heroic abnegation, the lover removing himself or herself for the sake of the loved one.

This certainly looks a little like loss of self, although the appearance may be misleading: the sublimation of the impulse to connect with the beloved might well result in stronger (but thwarted) feelings of this nature. More ordinary romantic love, in which romance goes smoothly so that connectedness and reciprocation are taken for granted, might yield something that more clearly resembles loss of self. Someone who loves loses his or her self in a kind of merging with the beloved.

What I want to argue is that the Bhagavad Gita could not possibly regard this as a workable solution to the problem of loss of self. This is because the loss of self is only partial, and in any case (like loss of self in sexual ecstasy) is only temporary. If the loss of self in romantic love were not merely partial, it would amount to the obsessive eroticism analyzed by de Rougemont, and in a way would be an extreme assertion of self rather than a genuine loss. Long-term love, on the other hand, is (as de Rougemont insists) very different. It involves something like parallel coordinated rhythms rather than immersion in the other.

The line of thought here is very much like one in Kierkegaard's *The Sickness Unto Death*. Kierkegaard thinks that there is a problem of self, although his view of what it is is certainly different from that of the Bhagavad Gita. What the two share is the insistence that, whatever the problem is, relationship with another finite being cannot completely or finally solve it. The absorption in, or anchoring to, another human can never be complete or strong enough.

A relationship with a divine being, though, is something else. For Kierkegaard this takes the form of faith, which Kierkegaard construes as a highly robust and pervasive personal attitude, in the God of Christianity. The Bhagavad Gita presents the option of devotion to a god or goddess. This devotion offers unlimited and unchanging possibilities of emotional self-abandonment, unlike any relation with another human being. The emotion of love and surrender is to involve no thoughts of future reward or reciprocation: the god or goddess is of course at a different level, removed from the devotee. The depth of love and surrender could not possibly be sustained over any period of time in relation to another finite being. But it is possible in relation to a god or goddess, and because of this such devotion ranks (alongside loss of self in meditative contemplation or in activity) as a permanent solution to the central problem of life.

In the abstract, any god or goddess will do as a target for unlimited devotion. Krishna modestly offers himself. One of the striking features of the Bhagavad Gita is that, while Krishna is the philosophical mouthpiece of the author (much like Socrates for Plato in the *Dialogues of Plato*), Krishna also displays himself as an attractive object of devotion. The display is variable, involving at least two separate presentations. It is not clear to me whether Krishna ever, in the Bhagavad Gita, appears as the handsome young, blue-skinned form that was later so widely represented in Indian art. This Krishna has two arms. The Bhagavad Gita makes clear that his form as a god features four arms. Finally, Krishna (unlike us) can manipulate his underlying identity with Brahman and actually give a visual presentation of this. At one point (The Eleventh Teaching) he does so, resulting in a stupendous vision of cosmic activity. Krishna (in Barbara Stoler Miller's brilliant translation) describes himself in this form as "time grown old" (p. 103), and in the end Arjuna begs him to resume his own four-armed form (p. 107).

Krishna's presentation of himself as Brahman is metaphysically consistent with the central vision of the Upanishads: that Brahman is everything. This is an unchanging truth. But the presentation is within the superficial framework, in which elements or aspects of Brahman that do change are evident as such. Time, with its destruction and creation, is very much part of the picture. This emphasis subtly alters the identification with the universe that is central to Hindu philosophy. It gives us identification with an explicitly active universe, in a way that parallels the new and attractive option of loss of self within activity.

Conclusion

The Bhagavad Gita gives us a view of the universe in which, as in the Upanishads, we are one with Brahman, which always remains Brahman. My suggestion is that this continuity of vision is presented with a change of tone and emphasis, so that the dynamic elements of the universe move to the foreground. The ethics of the Bhagavad Gita features a similar combination of continuity of central thesis, on one hand, and difference in ramifications, on the other.

Activity is seen as essential to life: even making oneself still and meditative is a form of activity. Krishna argues that nothing we do really makes a difference, so that activity that is infused with concern for reaching goals is seen as based on a delusion. Goal-directed activity is still possible; but it has validity only if it is something that you simply do, rather than its being driven by desire or anxiety. This gives us a morality in which one simply plays, with detachment, the role appropriate to one's caste. The warrior Arjuna will fight and kill; ideally he will lose himself in this activity and will not keep thinking about what the point of it is or about how it will end.

The larger part of the ethics of the Bhagavad Gita is concerned with the ethics of liberation. Liberation is distinct from moral virtue, although it presupposes it. In the religious system of Hinduism, the Law of Karma tells us that moral virtue will bring someone a favorable rebirth, whereas vice will bring rebirth in a lower caste or as an animal. Liberation, which is a matter of very good attitudes rather than merely meeting the general standards of good behavior, brings release from the wheel of rebirth. The liberated person enters *moksha,* which is thought of as an indescribable state. The Upanishads had insisted that it is not like waking consciousness or dreaming or dreamless sleep, although it is less unlike dreamless sleep than it is unlike the others.

The Bhagavad Gita presents the ideal of liberation in life in terms of a range of options. The Upanishads had insisted that the most desirable kind of life centered on a full, engrossing realization that *atman* is Brahman. This full realization required a withdrawal from normal social roles, and sustained involvement in a meditative and passive style of life. The centrality of the claim that *atman* is Brahman is retained in the Bhagavad Gita, which also agrees that an austere, meditative way of life can lead to the loss of self that is the appropriate response to this central claim.

But the Bhagavad Gita presents options that, it suggests, will be more attractive to most people. If all of life is activity, then the inner stasis so important to peace of mind and joy can be possible in the midst of energetic behavior just as well as in meditative retreat. Thus an enlightened and deeply satisfying life is possible within traditional role playing. What is crucial to the loss of self is a lack of concern for outcomes of the activity. This applies even to sacrifices to a god or goddess.

Devotion also can be a vehicle for loss of self. Lack of concern for outcome again is crucial. In practice, this requires an object of deep devotion that is not a fellow human being, in that surrender to love of a fellow human being almost inevitably brings with it concerns about the future. We care about the survival and well-being of the people we care for, and we also care about whether they will reciprocate our devotion. Hence, loss of self in deep devotion requires a god or goddess as an object of devotion.

Recommended Reading

The introduction to Barbara Stoler Miller's translation of the Bhagavad Gita (New York: Bantam Books, 1986) is very clear and useful.

Three entries in *A Companion to World Philosophies,* ed. Eliot Deutsch and Ron Bontekoe (Oxford: Blackwell, 1997), provide an especially useful contextual background in the history of Indian thought. They are Gerald James Larson, "Indian Conceptions of Reality and Divinity" (pp. 248–58); John M. Koller, "Humankind and Nature in Indian Philosophy" (279–89, especially 282–83); and J. N. Mohanty, "The Idea of the Good in Indian Thought" (290–303).

FOUR

CONFUCIUS

![ornament] For most Western readers the name Confucius conjures up a genre of jokes and anecdotes containing the words "Confucius says." The real Confucius is unknown, but the Confucius of pop culture is a pseudo–wise man (and part of the joke is that pop culture does not want to believe that anyone is really wise). This pseudo–wise man issues pithy sayings that sound like messages contained in demented fortune cookies.

The grain of truth in this image is that what survives of Confucius's thought consists entirely of pithy sayings, each of which could be squeezed into a fortune cookie. These fortune cookies, though, would produce puzzled looks rather than laughter. In most cases the saying, taken by itself, is pretty unintelligible, at least at first. You need to read a large number before many make much sense. If educated Chinese, Koreans, and Japanese (along with a small number of Western scholars) think that they understand *The Analects of Confucius*, it is because they have read it all, probably more than once. The pithy sayings take on meaning in the larger context.

For the Western reader who is not a specialist *The Analects of Confucius* initially will seem like one of those amorphous blots used in Rorschach tests. There may be patterns, but it looks as if it takes a lot of effort—and sheer imagination—to see any. This chapter is intended as an aid. We can group much of Confucius under the headings of major themes, locating passages in relation to these. What is to follow, then, is keyed to specific passages in the *Analects*, which can take on clear sense and also urgency. The translation used throughout is that of W. E. Soothill, for some time published by Oxford World's Classics, although there will be occasional comparisons with the competing versions of Arthur Waley and D. C. Lau, and also a new and very well received translation by Roger Ames and Henry Rosemont, Jr.

Confucius and *The Analects*

First, though, we need to know something about Confucius the man, and also about the one book we have of him. The dates usually assigned to Confucius are 551–479 BCE. This makes him a contemporary of Buddha in India, living more than a century before Socrates in Greece. China in this period was a chaotic patchwork of feudal kingdoms, with old memories of unifying empires. Every feudal ruler would have liked to conquer the others, reunifying the empire. Because how to do this was not entirely clear, a traveling philosopher like Confucius could gain an audience.

By our standards most of these feudal kingdoms were badly and selfishly governed. In bad years many of the peasants might starve. Confucius approached politics and government from a moral position. As he saw it, the ruler and his officials had strong obligations to the uneducated and unprivileged mass of the population. These began with seeing that they always had enough to eat, but went beyond this. Along with this moral position, Confucius had a personal ambition. His hope was that some ruler would appoint him as a government official with some real responsibility. Confucius then could create a demonstration model of good government that would transform China.

In the end he never got what he wanted, and the evidence is that he died thinking of himself as a failure. Like most failures, Confucius did other things while waiting for success. Principally he taught students, a group of young men who lived with him and traveled around China with him as his retinue.

Why did these young men come to study with Confucius? Probably there is no single answer. Confucius had the reputation of being wise, and also of being an expert on traditional Chinese culture (including *The Book of Songs,* folksong-like poems that have been translated by Arthur Waley and also by Ezra Pound). Undoubtedly some of his students were high-minded people who simply wanted to know more about such things. Some, however, must have been motivated by the hope of a lucrative and prestigious career as an official in some kingdom. Confucius taught the required skills, which included knowledge of the pervasive ritual that would be part of any job, as well as the cultural knowledge one might be expected to display and also rudimentary practical and political skills. A large part of what he taught was ethics; we can consider the importance of this for him (and his students) shortly.

The irony is that some of these students did get the coveted positions as government officials, even if Confucius himself never did. Perhaps Confucius seemed too serious and formidable. His students certainly would have seemed well trained. They also were trustworthy. Much as the professional ethics of a lawyer includes never breaching client confidentiality, the professional ethics of a government official (according to Confucius) included never participating in a rebellion, no matter how bad things got. A ruler could feel safe with these people.

As previously remarked, much of what Confucius taught was ethics: how to be a good person. For him this was one side of how to create good government, in that a good ruler (or official) works to benefit the people and also—in his goodness—serves as a role model that influences the character of the entire society. In some ways this sounds very "liberal," but Confucius had never heard of democracy and his model of good government was very paternalistic (the good rulers benefit the peasants, who really don't know much) rather than democratic. Perhaps we cannot expect even a great philosopher entirely to transcend the ethical limitations of his or her times. The possibility of democracy (which would have required a transformation of the population) never occurred to Confucius. For that matter women (in reality or as a topic) are almost entirely absent from *The Analects of Confucius*.

After Confucius died, his students collected what they remembered of his sayings, including in this also some sayings of leading students. The *Analects* is this collection. The version we have may date from as late as a century after Confucius's death.

The Ethical Ideal

Ethics is, in Confucius's view, central to everything that matters, including effective government. "He who governs by his moral excellence may be compared to the pole-star, which abides in its place, while all the stars bow toward it" (book 2, 1.). As Confucius knew, there is a lot more to effective government than being a good person, but he was convinced that no one could govern well who was not good. One reason was the subtle influence of the ruler, or the high official, as a role model, influencing the ways in which most people would think it seemed right to behave.

There are two questions in ethics that may or may not go together. One is "What is the best way to behave?" when making a moral or any other kind of choice. The other is "What is a good life, that is, one that is deeply satisfying and really worth having?" If you think that being a moral person is, as experienced from the inside, always wonderful, then you will think that these really are the same question, in two different forms. The great Greek philosopher Plato thought they were the same. If you think that moral people are sometimes unhappy, and that it often is not so wonderful from the inside, then you will have doubts. The great German eighteenth-century philosopher Immanuel Kant sounded skeptical, suggesting that (in this life at least) moral virtue correlates poorly with happiness. His strong recommendation of moral behavior was tied to its inherent dignity, not to any personal advantages.

Despite his own personal disappointments, Confucius seems much closer to Plato in his view of this than to Kant. He takes "What is a good life?" to be the most fundamental question of all. "What is the best way to behave?" is secondary. But there is a running argument that it is personally advantageous to be a truly virtuous person.

Our first fortune cookie on this subject is "A man without virtue cannot long abide in adversity, nor can he long abide in happiness; but the virtuous man is at rest in virtue, and the wise man covets it" (book 4, 2).

What does this mean? Well, everyone (even Confucius) has a chance of experiencing adversity. Projects fail. Hopes are disappointed. In the movies adversity for heroines and heroes does not last long, usually half an hour at most. But in real life adversity can go on for a long time. The word "abide" (Waley, and also Ames and Rosemont, have "endure" and Lau has "remain long") suggests the problem of long-term coping.

A lot depends on what matters most to you, and what your inner resources are. Someone who cares most about money and popularity can be devastated by becoming poor and friendless. Plainly what Confucius has in mind as a person with "virtue" is someone who will not be devastated whatever happens. Why not? Presumably the answer is that what matters most to such a person will not be things like money and popularity, which can be taken away suddenly by really bad luck. But if your major values include virtue itself—being a good person— then as long as you remain a good person, there will be something important to you that can't be taken away. With this source of satisfaction, you can abide in adversity.

It may seem puzzling that Confucius says that the man without virtue cannot long abide in happiness. Adversity is one thing, but you might think that anyone can endure happiness. However, if what makes you happy are things like money or success, the next question is "How much is enough?" A life that centers around these external values will be, almost necessarily, a life in which the person perpetually wants more. To "abide in happiness" (Ames and Rosemont have "enjoy happy circumstances for any period of time") requires that you be satisfied, that you not be prey to disruptive desires for more. These desires carry with them further risks, and anyway it is hard really to enjoy what you have if you are preoccupied with the dissatisfaction of not having as much as you now would like.

One thing that may make it hard to follow Confucius's thought here is that most of us know of (or can imagine) people who almost always do the right thing, and yet are crushed by adversity. In the Bible Job is such a character. Even if Confucius is right about how someone who is without virtue will not be able to abide in happiness, isn't he asking too much of the virtuous person?

Maybe. But there is one pithy saying that suggests Confucius's answer: "He who knows the truth is not equal to him who loves it, and he who loves it is not equal to him who delights in it" (book 6, 18). The idea seems to be that real virtue, of the first rank, involves an emotional satisfaction in itself. An idea like this occurs in some ancient Greek philosophy, notably that of Plato and Aristotle. It is connected with the claim that there is more to genuine virtue than merely a record of always doing the right thing: genuine virtue requires the right values and motivation, which would enable someone to do the right thing even in the sorts of difficult, tempting, or disorienting circumstances that most of us may never experience. Plato gestures toward this idea in his story in the *Republic* of the man who finds a ring of invisibility, who surely must come to realize that he can do anything he wants and get away with it. This would be a real test of virtue, and of what someone's real values are. A person who previously *seemed* virtuous might, as this man did, turn into a tyrant and a monster.

The explanation just completed, of how Confucius can hold that someone without virtue cannot long abide in adversity or in happiness, is intended to reveal the structure of his philosophy. It is sometimes said that Confucius is unlike most Western philosophers in not giving arguments for his views. There is some truth in this. Confucius, unlike his follower Mencius (see the next chapter), was not confronted with argumentative rival philosophers who created a pressing need to justify his views. So what emerges looks more like insights than arguments.

Nevertheless, there is an implicit structure of argument in Confucius. We have just seen an example of it. Unlike some philosophical arguments, it is not a closed loop of words. Instead it points outward, to general psychological facts about human life. The claims about people without virtue are supported by observation of the ways in which, for example, many who are given what they want become restless or bored. There is also the spine of coherence: Confucius's moral psychology of virtue is bolstered by the related conception of what true virtue is.

Let us return to Confucius's emphasis (shared with Plato and Aristotle) on inner satisfaction with one's own virtue, as a value. To some this smacks of narcissism. It seems to present true virtue as self-absorption. On the other hand, can anyone have a truly satisfying life who is not proud of something? And what more appropriate thing is there to be proud of than one's own better qualities, especially if these have not been won easily?

It is always tempting to view issues of this sort in terms of "Yes" or "No" answers. Is the idea of virtue as its own reward, in terms of psychological satisfaction, narcissistic or is it simply good sense? A better way, though, may be to see the issue in terms of a range of possibilities. After all, ideals always can become subtly corrupted. Something that is wonderful can have rotten look-alikes. So perhaps the relevant worry is whether the virtuous person remains to a large degree focused on the people who will benefit from the virtue, or whether the virtue turns *too* much inward?

Certainly virtuous behavior is, in Confucius's view, other-directed. The "one all-pervading principle" (book 4, 15) is "Conscientiousness within and consideration for others." Other people matter. They must be given consideration, but not necessarily in exactly the same way. Your parents matter in a way in which strangers do not. Political superiors (e.g., rulers, high officials) matter in a different way from the peasants. (We are repeatedly reminded that social equality would have seemed as alien and fantastic in Confucius's time as people flying would have.) In Waley's translation the all-pervading principle is "loyalty [for those above], consideration [for those below]."

Confucius regards your emotional states as significant, and he thinks that their connection with virtue is not random. "The noble man," he says, "is calm and serene, the inferior man is continually worried and anxious" (book 7, 36). Waley has "A true gentleman is calm and at ease; the Small Man is fretful and ill at ease." Ames and Rosemont (for whom it is 7, 37) have "The exemplary person is calm and unperturbed; the petty person is always agitated and anxious." Why is the inferior person prone to anxiety? The obvious answer is that if what you value most are "external" goods, such as money, outward success, and reputation—and if these are to some degree subject to "the luck of the draw"—then you have to worry about how lucky you will continue to be (or will become). Someone who places more emphasis on inner values will be less vulnerable to luck, and therefore can be more serene. The prevailing emotional cast in this view is the mark of accomplishment: "The enlightened are free from doubt, the virtuous from anxiety, and the brave from fear" (book 9, 28).

One of the disadvantages of philosophy as a compendium of pithy sayings is that each item is too short to admit of shadings and complications. We might wonder about the passage just cited. Aren't some people brave who do feel fear but overcome it? Shouldn't an enlightened person maintain an open mind, with some room for doubt? And couldn't a virtuous person sometimes experience genuine anxiety, say when threatened with imminent death?

In Confucius's case the shadings and complications are lateral. We need to go to other passages to find them. He never does take up the complications in what counts as courage, but there are many complicating comments on enlightenment and on what might disturb a virtuous person.

Indeed, there are repeated comments on what Confucius thought the limitations of his own enlightenment were. Apart from Socrates, it is hard to think of anyone who has come down to us as a major sage who was so alive to the possibility of making mistakes and was so open-minded as Confucius. He, the disciples report, "was entirely free from four things: he had no preconceptions, no pre-determinations, no obduracy, and no egoism" (book 9, 4). As he insists, "The wise man in his attitude towards the world has neither predilections nor prejudices" (4, 10).

There is always more to learn. One may learn from people who have very different points of view; there is always a chance that they have taken in something that one has missed. In book 18, 5–7, there are reports of encounters that Confucius and his students had with what sound very much like Daoists (Taoists), representatives of a great school of early Chinese philosophy (see chapters 6 and 7) opposed to what Confucius stood for. In two of the cases Confucius is anxious to talk with these people, to hear more of what they have to say; they for their part want nothing to do with Confucius and his followers.

With regard to virtue, there is an undercurrent of comment on how even someone who is genuinely virtuous can feel the tug of desires that bring some degree of disturbance or disappointment. Confucius never hid his disappointment at the failure to gain a responsible position as a high government official. There also is the comment that Confucius had never met a man whose love of virtue was as strong as his sexual desire (book 9, 17). He also observes that "wealth and rank are what men desire (but unless they be obtained in the right way they may not be possessed)" (book 4, 5). Plainly Confucius himself had these desires, although other values dominated them in his life.

The position seems to be that serenity is a matter of degree. Someone who is genuinely virtuous, in a way that involves valuing the inner harmony that virtue represents, will be significantly more serene than someone whose values are more heavily "external." But the serenity will hardly amount to being placid or smug. For that matter, a genuinely virtuous man should have some caution (although not outright anxiety) about his own virtue. Thus the disciple Tseng is quoted as saying "I daily examine myself on three points,—In planning for others have I failed in conscientiousness? In intercourse with friends have I been insincere? And have I failed to practise what I have been taught?" (book 1, 4).

The major complication of virtue that I think is inherent in Confucius's position goes beyond fallibility. It may be that virtues and what are faults always are intertwined in the same character. "A man's faults all conform to his type of mind. Observe his faults and you may know his virtues" (book 4, 7). Waley has "Every man's faults belong to a set [i.e., a set of qualities that includes virtues]. If one looks out for faults it is only as a means of recognizing Goodness." Lau has "In his errors a man is true to type. Observe the errors and you will know the man."

The natural thought, especially because Confucius repeatedly emphasizes his own limitations (and perhaps by implication the limitations of good people in general), is to turn the passage around and to suppose that if faults reveal likely virtues, virtues also reveal likely faults. Perhaps people tend to have the virtues of their faults, and the faults of their virtues? This line of thought certainly has occurred to some in the West, notably the great seventeenth-century master of pithy sayings, the Duc de La Rochefoucauld. La Rochefoucauld also provides the next step (maxim 182). If virtues and faults are intertwined, then it is easy to slip from virtuous to faulty behavior: self-monitoring and good practical sense are required in order to minimize this.

This observation may be related to a famous and puzzling comment that Confucius makes. "Your honest countryman," he says, "is the spoiler of morals" (book 17, 13). Waley has "The 'honest villager' spoils true virtue." This is usually interpreted, as Confucius's great fourth-century BCE follower Mencius did, in terms of the honest villager's poor motivation. That is, he wants too much to look good and to be approved. It may be also that part of the thought is that the honest villager's moral judgment will be reliable only in easy, garden-variety cases. In hard cases, whose features call for real thought, whatever virtues the villager has will slip into faults, including probably excessive rigidity and intolerance. Confucius emphasizes, contrasting himself with worthies of old who took rigid, high-minded stands, that "I am different from these. With me there is no inflexible 'thou shalt' or 'thou shalt not'" (book 18, 8). A truly virtuous person, unlike the honest villager, will be sensitive to the particular features of the case at hand. Nuances, which can include the style and attitude with which one acts, can make a great difference to the ethical quality of what is done.

My suggestion—it should be clear—is that Confucius's view of what it is to be a good person and to have a good life is both highly complex and also strenuous. It is not as if one becomes a good person and then can rest at entire ease for the remainder of one's life. The view is strenuous for the reader as well. No one passage, or even two or three passages, will give a large part of the view. Rather it emerges cumulatively from the entire *Analects*.

Becoming a Good Person

There also is a complex account of how someone becomes a very good person. The short version is "Let the character be formed by the poets; established by the laws of right behavior; and perfected by music" (book 8, 8). Waley's translation of this is helpfully more specific: "Let a man be first incited by the *Songs*, then given a firm footing by the study of ritual, and finally perfected by music."

Anyone who reads the *Book of Songs*, lovely and engaging as some of the poems are, may reasonably wonder what any of them has to do with ethics or virtue. The answer is that Confucius and his students read moral messages or hints about the good life into the poems, much as some readers find moral messages in the *I Ching* (*Book of Changes*), on the surface merely a manual of fortune-telling. An example of this kind of interpretation is book 3, 8, in which a student asks about the true meaning of a poem from the *Book of Songs*. The poem is ostensibly a description of a beautiful woman's face, speaking of dimples and her bewitching eyes, "Ground spotless and candid for tracery splendid!" Confucius's reply is "The painting comes after the ground-work," to which the student's quick reply is "Then manners are secondary?"

A good deal is striking in this highly condensed exchange. Both Confucius and the student know the Songs very well and are prepared to see hints in them about what has ethical importance. The exchange is an example of Confucius teaching, in which in fact the student takes the active role. The passage ends with Confucius's praise of the student. He is on record as saying that the kind of student he wants will be able, presented with one corner of a subject, to come back with the other three. Thus this kind of teaching is the opposite of "spoon feeding."

But what, one might ask, is the point? It is that manners are secondary to an initial phase of character formation, which lays the foundation for later refinements. There may be some analogy with Aristotle's view, in which phase 1 is an upbringing that instills good habits, along with a tendency to associate virtuous sorts of behavior with pleasure and inappropriate sorts with pain. Only someone who has had a good psychological foundation of this sort can be expected to be ready for Aristotle's lectures on ethics. These will inaugurate phase 2, in which one learns both to understand the point of virtue—to experience the point in appreciation of the inner harmony that true virtue involves—and also to use experience and judgment in solving the hard cases in which the best moral decision cannot simply be derived from a familiar general rule.

There is some analogy between Confucius's and Aristotle's views of ethical development, but also manifold differences. Aristotle emphasizes the importance of law in phase 1; Confucius, as we will see, is deeply skeptical about the uses of law. Nor does Confucius subscribe, as far as one can tell, to a psychology of habituated pleasure and pain. On the other hand, a large number of comments in the *Analects* about the importance of role models and such things as neighborly influences suggest that Confucius assumed that family and community relations would dominate phase 1. The differences between the two philosophers multiply in relation to phase 2. Confucius did take manners very seriously. We need to explore the roles he assigned to ritual, and also to music.

The emphasis on ritual may be, for many of us, the most indigestible element in Confucius's philosophy. Underlying this is a social divide. Confucius's society was extremely ritualized: ceremonies and proper ways of doing things pervaded the business of government and also had great importance in the lives of ordinary people. Contemporary Western societies, above all that of the United States, consider themselves largely free of such things, which are viewed as boring and intolerably artificial. Perhaps the sense of ritual that most of us retain centers on religious ceremonies, including weddings and funerals, and on legal proceedings.

On the other hand, there may be primitive rituals in our everyday lives that we do not think of as ritual. Saying "Thank you" for a present or a favor might be one example. Another is holding a door open for someone who is right behind you.

Part of our negative attitude to the idea of ritual stems from a sense that rituals are like magical formulas (except that really they change nothing, and thus are useless); the things that are supposed to matter in them include saying just the right words in the right order, and moving in the right direction at the right moment. The rituals that Confucius took seriously certainly would have had these qualities. But he repeatedly insists that a great deal beyond these features matters in the ritual. Style and demeanor, and, above all, the way in which what you do is connected with your attitudes, are most important.

This idea comes out most strongly in a discussion of ritual in 1, 12. The philosopher Yu is quoted as saying that what matters most in ritual is naturalness (Waley, Lau, and also Ames and Rosemont have "harmony"). There is, however, Yu observes, "a naturalness that is not permissible; for to know to be natural, and yet to be so beyond the restraints of decorum is also not permissible."

The translations "naturalness" and "harmony" are much closer than one might first think, if indeed naturalness is a matter of the way in which behavior harmonizes with one's attitudes and feelings. The idea is something like this. Ritual is a kind of social dance, in which people are constrained by established forms but at the same time do express themselves. If someone participates in a ritual that is meaningless to her or him, and feels nothing, then this ritual is empty and useless.

What is best is when someone, so to speak, "gets into" a ritual and makes of it a performance in which something genuine is well expressed. The ritual as a social dance may have the function of drawing people closer together, thereby strengthening a sense of community and encouraging feelings the opposite of loneliness and alienation. But it doesn't really work unless there is some sense of community to begin with, and there are some appropriate attitudes and feelings already.

Ritual refines the self. This is brought out in a passage in which a student asks Confucius about "the man who is poor yet not servile, or who is rich yet not proud." He will do, replies Confucius, "but he is not equal to the man who is poor and yet happy, or rich and yet loves courtesy." The student then shines by quoting a relevant passage from the *Book of Songs:* "Like cutting, then filing; Like chiselling, then grinding." He offers this as an interpretation of what Confucius has just said. The passage (book 1, 15) ends with Confucius's making an appreciative comment on the student.

Cutting, filing, chiseling, and grinding all are metaphors for the refinement of what is already pretty good. We might use the metaphor of fine-tuning. The practice of ritual, and also music, will work for someone who is already a pretty good person, or at least is well on the way to being a good person. Both ritual and music supply forms that help to structure emotional patterns and movement of the body, and thus help to turn what is roughly right into a personality that is very right.

This, then, is an ethics that links being the best kind of person with culture. A natural response might be that, while culture may be nice, true goodness is a kind of inner quality that does not need refinements. This response shows up in the *Analects*. A local high official remarks to one of Confucius's students that "For a man of high character to be natural is quite sufficient; what need is there of art to make him such?" The student responds that "Art, as it were, is nature; as nature, so to speak, is art. The hairless hide of a tiger or leopard is about the same as the hide of a dog or a sheep" (Book 12, 8). The immediate point is that perhaps, underneath it all, we (including heroes, villains, nice people, and mean people) are much the same, but this means rather little in relation to actual virtue. There also is the point that the culture and refinement that shape us become second nature.

Music also is important in shaping us, especially our patterns of emotional response. Music is more than bells and drums (book 17, 11). The sounds and the movements of performers are certainly part of it, but the meanings and attitudes that the music involves are far more important than the bare physical ingredients. Thus it is that Confucius in several passages comments (as Plato also does) on the kinds of music that are good in psychic development and the kinds that he thinks are bad. We know that Confucius himself played a string instrument. Good music was, from his point of view, a pleasure; but it was more than a pleasure, having real ethical importance.

There is an amusing passage that shows how much the importance of music was taken for granted in Confucius's circle and also sheds light on the kind of relationship Confucius enjoyed with his students. One of them has been given a coveted official position, governorship of a small walled town. As part of strengthening civic goodness, he (in something that sounds straight out of Monty Python) promotes musical performances. Confucius, coming for a visit, hears everywhere the sound of string instruments and singing. He teases his disciple, comparing all of this to using an ox-cleaver to kill a chicken, but has to admit that there is some basis in his philosophy for this policy.

Law

The example just used, of music employed to boost civic excellence, may seem bizarre partly because one of our standard ideas of how civic excellence can be boosted centers on law, not music. We think that good laws can increase the incidence of virtue within the population. Confucius certainly has nothing against good laws and does not for a moment believe that a viable society can do without law. Nevertheless, the role he assigns to law is relatively minor, and he would be skeptical about the Western emphasis on it.

Thus he remarks (book 12, 13), "I can try a lawsuit as well as other men, but surely the great thing is to bring about that there be no going to law." This concerns civil law, and one might think that what is most ethically important is criminal law. But here again Confucius would like to marginalize the use of law. "If you govern the people by laws, and keep them in order by penalties," he says (book 2, 3), "they will avoid the penalties, yet lose their sense of shame." The alternative is "[I]f you govern them by your moral excellence, and keep them in order by your dutiful conduct, they will retain their sense of shame, and also live up to this standard."

Here again we encounter a political vision that is heavily oriented toward the well-being of the common people but also highly paternalistic. The ruler and his officials set the tone of the society, and by their virtues (including a visible sense of responsibility for the good of the peasants) should establish models that will ensure that the society is harmonious. There are two parts to this recipe for the civic virtue of the common people. They require good models above them. But they also have to have enough to eat. It may be too much to expect civic virtue if there is a shortage of food. For all of these reasons the ruler who wishes to create a law-abiding polity in which people trust their rulers has a first priority of seeing that the people have enough to eat. This comes even before education and culture (book 12, 7).

A really good person, in Confucius's view, will not resort to crime even when short of food. A standard view in our time is that people are, by and large, either good or bad, with perhaps room for a fair number of borderline cases. Confucius's view seems to have been that truly good people are uncommon, and it is likely that he would have said the same thing about truly bad people. The great majority of people, including the "honest villager" and virtually all of the peasants, are neither truly good nor truly bad. In this Confucius subscribes to a map of goodness and badness in the population in some respects like that developed by Plato about a century later, one that is also supported by research in contemporary social psychology that suggests that most people are heavily "situational" in their good or bad behavior.

Certainly Confucius's view of ordinary people is that what we can expect from them depends very much on the situations they are in. Important relevant factors in his view will include the models supplied by the leaders of society, and also whether life can seem moderately satisfactory if one remains virtuous. The common people, Confucius suggests, can be made to follow a proper way of life; they cannot be made to understand it (book 8, 9). The passage immediately after that observes that "One who is by nature daring and is suffering from poverty will not be law-abiding" (Waley translation).

Thus widespread crime and wrongdoing have to be seen as symptomatic of social evils such as poverty. In some ways this may look very much like what we are familiar with as a contemporary liberal view of crime. However, as we shortly will see, Confucius was not exactly "soft" on crime, whatever he thought about the causes of widespread crime. He did have a sense that bad societal leadership has to bear the primary responsibility for outbreaks of crime. There is a dramatic expression of this in an exchange Confucius had with the dictator of his home state of Lu. This worthy complained that there was an outbreak of robbery; Confucius (who was risking his neck in saying this) replies, "If you, Sir, be free from the love of wealth, although you pay people, they will not steal" (book 12, 18). In other words, the example of greed at the top contributes to crime. Confucius then risks his neck again, countering the suggestion that perhaps capital punishment would solve the problem by remarking that there is no need for that. What is crucial is the example the ruler sets.

Confucius definitely did believe that criminals, whatever the social conditions that led to their actions, should be punished. A negative comment on "petty acts of clemency" (book 15, 16, Waley's translation) makes this clear. He may well have believed also that there will be some criminals even in the best-governed society. So we need the protection of law. All the same, in his view frequent and heavy-handed legal compulsion is a sign that the ruling group is either ineffective or full of corrupt desires. An analogy might be with a teacher's uses of discipline in a schoolroom full of young children. It can be a sign of inexperienced or poor teaching if discipline is constantly accentuated. Conversely, a skilled teacher who is like a polestar to the class will normally (barring unusually difficult conditions surrounding the classroom) have little need for this.

The Good Ruler

The major requirement for a good ruler is to be a good person. There may also be an element of projection that goes beyond being an ordinary good person. The analogy with the polestar might suggest that the example that the ruler provides should not only be good but also should shine.

This may seem like a naive reduction of politics to morality. Confucius makes abundantly clear, however, that there are essential skills involved in being a good ruler or a good official. Merely being a thoroughly decent, well-meaning person is hardly enough. There is, first of all, the fact that the ruler and officials are parts, so to speak, of a management team; and the development and shaping of this team are crucial to success. Thus Confucius tells various rulers (book 2, 19–20) that it is important to promote the right people, and also to instruct officials who need to gain competence. Further it is not enough to be well-meaning: work must get done promptly and efficiently. There must be "economy in expenditure," and the people must be employed "on public works at the proper seasons" (book 1, 5).

The point of this last remark might escape someone who was unfamiliar with the workings of agricultural societies. In earlier times it had been common around the world for peasants (in the absence of construction firms or of a corps of public employees) to be required to engage in road building and maintenance, and in other public works projects. This was a form of taxation in work rather than in money. This requirement could be ruinous for peasants if it interfered with sowing or with harvesting, and would be much less damaging at times less suitable for agricultural work. Hence a smart official should know "the proper seasons" for demanding public works activity from the peasants.

This example separates the criteria for being a good official or ruler from the criteria for personal virtue. Skill and practical knowledge are required, above and beyond goodness. However, the separation may not be as great as one might think. A lot depends on what one thinks the standards are for personal virtue.

Many people regard good intentions—that is, meaning well—as crucial. But "meaning well" can be compatible with carelessness or sloppiness that, on the part of someone who has real responsibilities, can lead to a great deal of suffering. Think of a "well-meaning," but thoughtless or inexperienced, official who insists that the peasants build roads during the harvest season, thus contributing to a food shortage that causes much misery. Confucius, I believe, would say that a truly good person would not be thoughtless in something that mattered and would also take the trouble to find out relevant facts. Genuine virtue, then, would include being careful and thorough. In this sense being truly good goes far beyond "meaning well."

Why would an inexperienced official go to the trouble to find out what would matter most to the peasant population he controls? The answer lies in the "love of the people" mentioned immediately after "economy of expenditure" in book 1, 5 as a characteristic of a good ruler or official. To love or to care is not merely to have feelings. Indeed, feelings may be only a small part of it. A larger part typically will be attentiveness and concern, as evinced in doing what it takes to benefit those one cares about. Thus the bottom line for the good ruler is benefit for the people.

Conclusion

At the heart of Confucius's philosophy is a vision of the individual (even the ruler or high official) as enmeshed in a society. The strongest points of connection will be those of family. Given this vision, we are supposed to see that the most satisfying, as well as the most virtuous, kind of life involves active responsibility for others. This social dimension is crucial to a good life. To be entirely separate from one's societal connections would be like being a fish out of water.

There may be some contrast here with the way in which many people in our society think about life. It is often remarked that modern Western views of the self tend to be highly individualistic. People frequently claim to be able to imagine themselves, without any difficulty or sense of likely strain, as transported to a different kind of society or even a different time while remaining very much the same person. (This expectation that one would remain the same person in any context, it should be emphasized, reveals a *view* of what the self is. The realities might turn out to be very different.)

It is sometimes suggested that this vision of selfhood, which highlights a kind of disconnectedness and autonomy, is much more common among men than among women. This is one of the apparent implications of Gilligan's study, *In A Different Voice,* which contrasts female and male approaches to moral decision making. A number of commentators have pointed out that the self of the Confucian tradition, even though it is the product of a patriarchal society, does not fit this contrast. It is distinguished by its embeddedness in family and community, and lacks the radical individualism sometimes found in the West.

We have seen that Confucius believed that an educated and morally committed elite should take a leadership role in society, ideally filling positions as government officials. We have also seen that literary classics (in Confucius's day including most notably the *Songs*) played a major role in the training of this elite. These disparate elements came together in the triumph of Confucianism during the Han dynasty, nearly three centuries after Confucius's death. It was decided in 196 BCE that the highly prestigious jobs as government officials would be filled as a result of competitive examinations. What would the examinations test? In the light of Confucius's career the answer must have seemed obvious. The examinations would be largely keyed to the classics of Chinese literature. It was as if coveted positions in our government were filled by examinations keyed to Shakespeare and Milton. (There is an excellent account of some examination questions in Arthur Waley's biography of the great ninth-century poet Po Chu-i.) The Chinese civil service that developed was far in advance of anything comparable elsewhere in the world. It also led to the long-term dominance of a scholar elite over Chinese culture and society.

Nevertheless, it may be oversimple to speak of the triumph of

Confucianism. There were other strong currents in Chinese society. When Buddhism arrived from India a few hundred years later, it exerted a strong influence. Even before that, Daoism (which we will begin to look at in chapter 6) was a major rival of Confucian thought. The distinguished historian of Chinese philosophy Fung Yu-lan has suggested that after a certain point many educated Chinese combined Confucianism and Daoism in their lives. A nice example of combination is provided by the two happy endings of the great eighteenth-century Chinese novel that has been translated under the title *Story of the Stone,* and also has been translated as *Dream of the Red Chamber.* The hero unexpectedly does extremely well on the civil service exams (a Confucian happy ending, in which he brings honor to his entire family), and then for mystical purposes disappears from the world (a combined Buddhist and Daoist happy ending).

Recommended Reading

Herrlee Glassner Creel, *Chinese Thought from Confucius to Mao Tse-tung* (Chicago: University of Chicago Press, 1953) is a highly readable general introduction to the history of Chinese philosophy.

Fung Yu-Lan, *A Short History of Chinese Philosophy,* ed. Derk Bodde (New York: Free Press, 1948) is an extremely well-regarded standard history.

David Hall and Roger Ames, *Thinking Through Confucius* (Albany: State University of New York Press, 1987) is a good general guide to Confucius's thought.

Philip J. Ivanhoe, *Confucian Moral Self Cultivation* (Indianapolis: Hackett, 2000) examines the central theme of the philosophy of Confucius and his school.

Roger Ames, "The Chinese Conception of Selfhood," in *A Companion to World Philosophies,* ed. Eliot Deutsch and Ron Bontekoe (Oxford: Blackwell, 1997), 148–54, usefully explores a topic of special importance.

FIVE

MENCIUS

 Mencius was a Confucian philosopher of the fourth century BCE, living nearly two centuries after Confucius and a near-contemporary of Aristotle in Greece. He is one of those philosophers who is best known for a single, tenaciously argued claim. His philosophy, looked at closely, contains fascinating detail—straddling the border between philosophy and psychology—on what is involved in becoming a really good person.

The central claim is sometimes rendered as "Human nature is good." Some modern thinkers have maintained this position in an extreme form: society corrupts people and promotes selfish behavior, but in a simpler, natural state these people would be peaceful and cooperative. Ideas of this sort have been associated with romanticism and the legend of the "noble savage," and also with anarchism (the political philosophy that rejects the authority of governments). The extreme opposite of this optimism is the view that there is something potentially nasty in human nature, which urgently needs to be kept under control. This pessimism about human nature is dramatized in a well-known novel, William Golding's *Lord of the Flies,* which chronicles the behavior of a group of schoolboys shipwrecked on a deserted island and thus removed from normal restraints.

Mencius certainly is not a pessimist about human nature, but neither does he share the extreme optimism sometimes associated with romanticism or with anarchism. His thesis is that there is an innate *element* of benevolence (really, of benevolent *urges*) in human beings. Because the claim concerns an element of human nature, rather than a tendency that necessarily is dominant, it leaves room for other powerful elements of human nature, including of course selfishness.

The thesis of innate benevolence was new. There is no clear evidence that Confucius held such a view. Nevertheless, Mencius is very Confucian in continuing the master's twin preoccupations with the process that makes someone a very good person, and with the links between personal goodness and good government. Xunzi, (Hsun-Tzu), who lived in the century after Mencius, was Mencius's great adversary within Confucianism. Xunzi, in opposition to Mencius's insistence that humans are innately inclined toward benevolence, argued that human nature (at least at the start) is ethically inadequate. This argument is sometimes portrayed as flat opposition: Mencius holds that human nature is good, and Xunzi holds that it is evil. But most commentators now agree that Mencius and Xunzi are not as opposed as that makes them sound. Xunzi wanted to emphasize the artificial, learned character of morality; and for Mencius too there was certainly a gap between benevolent impulses (the sprouts of morality, in his view) and being a genuinely moral person.

Much of Mencius's philosophy arranges itself around his central thesis, and the need to defend it against the attacks of anti-Confucian schools of philosophers that had developed in China by the fourth century BCE. Some difficulties are dealt with at length. With regard to some problems, Mencius's views are merely a matter of conjecture. Here is a sampling of the questions that naturally occur in relation to the view that human nature has an innate element of benevolence:

1. What evidence, if any, is there for such a claim?
2. Does the claim amount to saying that there is a fixed element in human psychology throughout a person's entire life?
3. If human nature is innately benevolent, how is it that most human behavior is not especially benevolent, even in situations in which benevolence is called for?
4. How is it that there are cruel or selfish human beings that appear to have not a shred of benevolence in their makeup?
5. If there is an innate element of benevolence, how can individuals be made to develop this into full-fledged moral virtue?

Defending the Claim of Innate Benevolence

Mencius treats his central thesis as at bottom empirical. This should not lead us to expect that everyone will agree on it. Empirical investigations often are more complex and open to debate than most of us would like to believe. Scientists, even in our time, do often argue among themselves. Much, it turns out, depends on what one looks for and how one proceeds in looking for it. Often it appears that the structure of the investigation has a good deal to do with the results that it yields, and that two competent scientists who investigate in different ways can come up with different results.

This is true even for such "hard" sciences as physics and chemistry. The latitude for interpretation of results is especially broad in psychology, and there are special philosophical issues concerning psychological evidence. How much should one rely on introspection, bearing in mind that this risks basing one's psychological knowledge on a single case (one's own)? How much weight can be placed on other people's reports of what they think or feel, bearing in mind that people often lack self-knowledge and view themselves in an excessively favorable light? Beyond these problems of evidence there is a special complication in psychological investigations related to ethics. Ethical judgments are likely to enter in at the fundamental level. For example, if we are trying to generalize about the psychology of virtue, we first have to decide what our standards are for virtue, and that is an ethical question. If we wish psychological understanding of what it is to have a wonderful and exemplary life, we need to make some value judgments of what kinds of life are wonderful and exemplary.

Because of this interpenetration of philosophy and psychology, there is an area of study—moral psychology—in which the two cannot readily be disentangled. There are some modern Western philosophers (David Hume and Friedrich Nietzsche are examples) who can be read either as philosophers or as psychologists, although really they are both. There is a great deal of moral psychology both in Mencius and in Confucius.

Mencius appeals to two sources of evidence for the thesis of innate benevolence. One is that there are unexpected flashes of what looks like benevolent thought and behavior that cannot plausibly be explained in terms of self-interest. These suggest that, even if almost all of us are occupied most of the time in particular projects and in self-interest, there is something else—benevolence—in our makeup that manifests itself clearly at odd moments.

The other source of evidence is a thought experiment (i.e., an experiment one imagines rather than actually performing). Mencius's experiment (book 2, A.6) involves a young child who is about to fall into a well (which presumably will be fatal). Anyone, Mencius suggests, would wish to save the child, whether or not she or he wished to gain praise or reward. Suppose that someone has absolutely nothing to gain by rescuing the child or to lose by watching it die (we may imagine someone who is about to leave the area and will be far removed from any positive or negative consequences). The suggestion is that just about anyone—even, say, a petty criminal—would save the child.

David Hume, who also advanced a thesis of innate benevolence, suggested (two thousand years after Mencius) a similar thought experiment in his *Enquiry Concerning the Principles of Morals.* Hume's concerned gout, a painful disease that particularly attacked and sensitized the feet. No one, Hume claimed, would deliberately step on someone's gouty toes rather than stepping to the side.

Thought experiments are not real experiments, and some might prefer to set up a number of experimental subjects walking toward purportedly gouty feet (or watching small children seemingly about to fall into wells). My guess, though, is that most people would expect the results of real experiments to match those that Mencius and Hume assign to their thought experiments. This all seems interesting and important. But what exactly, one might ask, does it prove? Here the philosophical element in moral psychology comes to the fore.

Mencius and Hume certainly cannot be said to share a philosophy. Despite some striking similarities, they have different philosophical concerns, keyed to different contexts of inquiry. Hume is preoccupied (in the ethical parts of his writing) with a contrast between reason and sentiment as rival linchpins of ethical judgments, and also with a running polemic against his predecessor Thomas Hobbes's view of human nature and the origin of society. Mencius has no concerns that closely correspond to these, but conversely is strongly committed (in a way Hume is not) to exploring the moral psychology of how someone is to become a really good person. Mencius can analyze this moral development only if he first becomes clear about what is present (and what is absent) at the starting point.

My reading of Mencius is that, while his most dramatic claim concerns what is present at the starting point (i.e., benevolent urges), he was most concerned about what was absent. We, however, can focus on the notion of innate benevolence and ask what it means. Let us take this one word at a time. What does "innate" mean? What is benevolence?

In Western philosophy innateness has a long history, in which major figures include Plato (who flourished about half a century before Mencius) and the seventeeth-century French philosopher René Descartes. The contemporary linguist Noam Chomsky has argued that structures of language are in some sense innate. In Plato's dialogue *Meno,* the idea is floated that some kinds of knowledge (e.g., of mathematics) are innate in that they represent reminiscence from a previous life.

This almost certainly was intended as mythic and suggestive rather than as literal truth. Taken in the most simple way as literal truth, it could be funny. The nineteenth-century poet Shelley, having read Plato, wandered around Oxford interrogating babies about their innate ideas. They refused to speak to him. According to the *Oxford Book of Literary Anecdotes,* he complained to a friend "How provokingly close are these new-born babies! But it is not the less certain, despite the cunning attempts to conceal the truth, that all knowledge is reminiscence."

If there are innate ideas, it makes sense to regard them as capacities or propensities rather than as fully formed ideas in very young children. Then we would interpret theses of innate ideas as actually positing psychological vectors that will be activated at various levels of development. "Innate" then means something like "preset."

Is benevolence innate in this way? The psychologist Martin L. Hoffman has experimentally determined that there are to be found, even in very young children, patterns of empathetic distress responding to the distress of others. This is of course first and foremost empathy of response; benevolence of behavior may raise more complicated issues. But Hoffman's data do suggest independent support for something like Mencius's thesis.

"What is benevolence?" may look like a silly question. But think of what is involved in giving money to an alcoholic or a drug addict, or of the case of a doctor who insists on sticking a needle (containing an inoculation) into the arm of a crying child. Then there are the more complicated cases in which loving parents give freely of whatever a child wants, and in the process impair the child's ability to cope with the challenges of life.

The impulses of benevolence have a great deal to do with making people happy, giving them what they want, and preventing harm. But then there is the further question "Is what is meant to be benevolent really benevolent: does it really benefit the recipient?" Some knowledge of how the world works, often including knowledge of the conventions of society within which actions have their effects, usually is required to answer this. Value judgments, say of whether what feels good is genuinely worthwhile, also can play a part. In simple cases, as when someone is saved from drowning or protected from a random beating, it is usually clear that what is intended as benevolent really is. There are more elaborate cases that require more knowledge of the social machinery and of the world.

In any law case, is it genuinely benevolent (and praiseworthy) for a judge to award money to people because they are very nice and need the money? One needs here not only a sense of how the law works but also of the likely effects of the sort of legal generosity that this action would involve. Some of these effects very probably would be unfortunate, undermining people's ability to trust legal entitlements that we often depend upon. Viewed within the larger context, what the "benevolent" judge did would seem silly and harmful rather than benevolent.

Because of the differences among cases, Hume distinguished between "natural" virtues, such as kindness and compassion, and "artificial" virtues, such as justice. The latter require a knowledge of social conventions that the former do not need. Although Mencius does not formulate any such distinction, he is aware that what looks or feels benevolent may not be genuinely benevolent. He gives an example (book 4, B.2) of a high official who on occasion lends his carriage to help people ford local rivers. But he could have built footbridges. What looked and undoubtedly felt benevolent was not genuinely so, if one considers what a truly effective policy of helping people would be like.

Mencius's best example of a flash of benevolent thought and behavior concerns a king (book 1, A.7) who had spared a sacrificial ox. He had seen the animal's fear as it was on its way to be killed and out of sympathy preserved its life. The story is, however, less upbeat than, wrenched out of context, it might seem. In the first place, the ceremony required the sacrifice of an animal, and hence a lamb (whom the king did not see) was dispatched in the ox's place. Second, Mencius points out to the king that, as a result of his thoughtless economic policies, peasants are suffering and sometimes are on the verge of starvation. Even if we put to the side the unseen lamb that died, we need to juxtapose the king's genuine benevolence to the ox with his effects on the lives of the peasants (who are largely unseen by him).

All of this connects with Mencius's greatest preoccupations: (1) How is it that the great majority of human beings are not consistently or thoroughly benevolent? and (2) How can people morally improve? Before we look into these matters though, we need to pursue Mencius' positive thesis. We have already been looking at his evidence for innate benevolence. This evidence is supplemented by a case for regarding benevolence as normally a fixed element in the human psyche.

Benevolence as Essential to Being Human

There are two passages that especially develop this case. One is an argument against the skeptical view, advanced by some anti-Confucian philosophers, that morality goes against human nature. Mencius argues (book 6, A.1) that the process of becoming moral is hardly one in which normal instinctual life is bent entirely out of shape. Further, insofar as morality is directed toward benefiting the human race, there is a natural orientation toward it, like that of water seeking its own level. Mencius's argument here seems to appeal to the experience of becoming moral, insisting that it will be experienced as a fulfillment of some of our basic impulses rather than as repressive and unnatural. Plainly the argument makes sense only if one thinks in terms of a morality that is socially concerned and designed to promote happiness, and that leaves plenty of room for normal instinctual satisfactions.

The second passage (book 7, A.1) appeals to what will be involved in experiences of self-fulfillment. In the translation by D. C. Lau it goes "For a man to give full realization to his heart is for him to understand his own nature, and a man who knows his own nature will know Heaven." Mencius goes on to suggest that this is a matter of retaining benevolence as well as understanding it, and of serving heaven as well as knowing it.

Most readers new to Chinese philosophy will see a passage like this as bland and as quasi-religious. Arguably it is neither, but one has to appreciate a set of connected assumptions in much early Chinese philosophy in order to understand this. Early Chinese thought contained no clear position, positive or negative, in relation to a supreme being. Confucius refused to offer opinions on what we might think of as religious issues. Because of this feature of Confucianism, Matteo Ricci, the great seventeenth-century Jesuit who stayed in China and immersed himself in Chinese culture, saw no conflict between Confucianism (which he respected) and his brand of Christianity.

Tian (t'ien), which is generally translated as "heaven," refers to a kind of impersonal—but not morally neutral—cosmic order, which manifests itself especially in natural and political disasters that undermine wicked rulers. The assumption is that the universe has as it were its own purposes. Insofar as we are part of the universe, we can be attuned to the purposes of *tian*. Or, like the wicked rulers, we can be deeply opposed to these purposes.

This is an element in early Confucian thought that cannot be ignored, although on the whole it is far less prominent than are analyses of human behavior and growth that we might think of as naturalistic. It also may remind some readers who already know something about Daoism (Taoism; to be examined in the next two chapters) of the characteristic strong Daoist emphasis on harmony between human beings and the cosmic order. This element in Daoism goes far beyond anything in Confucianism, but even an extremely slight similarity provides yet one more reason to regard Confucianism and Daoism as not diametrically opposed.

When Mencius claims that to give full realization to your heart is to understand not merely your own nature but also *tian,* he is arguing that your nature, like *tian,* is not morally neutral. The analogy is worth taking seriously. The cosmic order certainly is not such that all stories have happy endings. Good people get horrible diseases; wickedness sometimes triumphs; and even good rulers sometimes experience bad harvests and the occasional flood. The standard early Chinese assumption is that the way the world works is a welter of good, bad, and indifferent but, nevertheless, that at some crucial moments (such as the fall of a dynasty) there is a tilt against wickedness. In much this way, it is reasonable to read Mencius as holding that the normal impulses of the average human being are a mixture of good, bad, and indifferent. There is benevolence, but there is much besides. Nevertheless, benevolence is special, and at certain crucial moments (as when the small child is about to fall into the well) there is a tilt in the direction of goodness.

Plainly it helps to be in touch with (so to speak) your benevolence. Mencius's language seems to suggest that the experience that this will yield will be satisfying rather in the way in which a natural expression of deep inner impulses is satisfying. You will feel good about yourself and feel more like a complete human being, he suggests, if you nurture your nature.

The argument (if this reading is correct) is something like the following.

When you act benevolently, it will feel good; it will feel like self-realization.

It wouldn't feel that way if benevolence weren't part of your nature.

All of this is part of a universal human experience connected with acting benevolently.

Therefore benevolence is not merely part of your nature; it is part of human nature.

Explaining Failures to Behave Benevolently

If Mencius is right in thinking that human nature is benevolent, then how is it that we sometimes fail to act benevolently, in situations in which we could help others or prevent harm to them? The simplest explanation is that benevolence is not all of human nature; selfish impulses or the demands of particular projects can outweigh benevolence. This, however, would not explain cases in which benevolent impulses are not present at all. We are left with the question of why benevolence flickers only occasionally in the mind of people like the king who spared the ox.

Mencius's answer is in part that the circumstances of life affect what comes to mind and how we think of it. Even a person's occupation matters. Thus (book 2, A.7) an armor maker is likely to be oriented to benevolence, in the form of preventing harm, much more than the arrow maker. Whom we talk with, and what is treated as normal and reasonable, also will make a difference to the presence or absence of benevolent impulses in our thinking. The balance of influences is crucial. This is an important feature of the role of parents, of course. But it also should be decisive (book 3, B.6) in the selection of teachers and of those who will surround and advise a king.

There is an elitism in Mencius's thinking about failures of benevolence, despite his apparently egalitarian insistence that all humans share benevolence as part of their original nature. Perhaps we all share it, but some lapse or lose it more readily than others. The contrast in this way of thinking is between the common person and the "gentleman." This sounds like a straightforward distinction of social class. But one needs to be mindful that what Confucians mean by a "gentleman" is fundamentally connected with refinement, so that it is always imaginable that someone wealthy and powerful will not be a "gentleman." A poor scholar, on the other hand, may well be a "gentleman."

The contrast and also the possible tenuousness of benevolence come out clearly in book 4, B.19 where Mencius says that human beings and brute beasts are not so far apart in their natures. Whatever the difference is, common people tend to lose it while the right kind of person retains it. (This bleak view of the average person may look more understandable if one imagines a primitive agricultural society in which the vast majority of people are peasants with no real education, who most years are struggling merely to stay alive.) There is in what Mencius says some echo of Confucius's view that someone who has internalized goodness can be relied on to be virtuous even in dire poverty, whereas a ruler who wants the great majority of people to behave virtuously had better make sure that they are not too badly off. The virtuousness of the average person, in this skeptical view, comes and goes according to circumstances and hence is not true virtue.

Along these lines Mencius remarks (book 6, A.7) that in good years (presumably ones with good harvests) most of the young men will be lazy, whereas in bad years one has to worry about violence. Perhaps this reflects basic human nature, although some people (the "gentlemen") then do develop in admirable ways. Mencius goes on to compare the circumstances of life with the soil in which plants grow. Favorable influences and instruction are like rich soil. They can produce even a sage who is in touch with the benevolence in his heart. Less favorable circumstances will produce people whose incidence of virtuous behavior can vary from year to year.

Beyond all of this, there is one factor in failures of benevolence that Mencius does not mention explicitly but is implicit in some of what he says. This is simple thoughtlessness, of the "Out of sight, out of mind" variety. Most of us can readily fail to be benevolent to people we do not see, perhaps because they are far away or for some other reason. This is noticeable in the story of the king who spared the ox whose fear he saw, but who cheerfully then consigned to sacrifice a lamb he did not see. The same king's policies also consigned many of his people to want and misery, but presumably he hardly saw that as well.

It would be nice to believe that hardly anyone would fail in benevolence to someone whose misery she or he would witness, but there is plenty of evidence to the contrary. A weaker claim, which seems much more plausible, is that most people find it easier to fail in benevolence if they do not witness the sufferings of those they fail. It may be easier to burn someone to death by dropping something from an airplane than it would be if one were looking in the victim's eyes. Similarly, it is much easier to ignore someone starving to death if the victim is thousands of miles away rather than in the same room or on the same sidewalk. There is no doubt that, as Jonathan Bennett pointed out in a Tanner Lecture, our consciences tend to be keener when we can visualize, as it were, a parade of those we have failed or wronged than when those we have failed or wronged are people we are hardly acquainted with and perhaps have not seen.

Total Loss of Benevolence

People for whom benevolence flickers now and then, and often fails, are regarded by Mencius as (regrettably) normal cases. Their moments of benevolence do testify to its place in human nature. The really troubling cases are those in which benevolence seems to have disappeared totally from someone's makeup. How can this be, if benevolence is essential to human nature?

David Hume (who, as we have seen, held a view similar to Mencius's) had a simple and direct way of saving the thesis that benevolence is essential to humanity. If what is said about the Emperor Nero (who showed no tincture of benevolence) is true, Hume contends, then he had lost his humanity. Similarly, the ancient Scythians, who took scalps, had lost their humanity.

This move ensures that apparent counterexamples do not actually count against the thesis that links humanity and benevolence. The fuller significance of Hume's maneuver can be appreciated if one bears in mind that for him, as indeed for Confucius and Mencius, humanity had somewhat the central role in ethics that duty later had for the German philosopher Immanuel Kant. Indeed, for Confucius especially, the central examples of moral failure will involve failure to respond with human-heartedness, whereas for Kantians they will be failures to adhere to the rules built into a practice (e.g., making false promises, taking someone else's property). Of course, Confucians condemn theft and Kantians condemn unkindness; the point is that the two moral views nevertheless have different preoccupations and different ways of modeling virtue.

For Mencius, in any event, total loss of benevolence is a loss of humanity. But the interesting question, from his point of view, is how it can happen. How can something that is essential to human nature totally drop out?

There is one elaborate discussion of this, in which Mencius (characteristically) uses a horticultural metaphor. He speaks of Ox Mountain, where once the trees were luxuriant (book 6, A.8). But they were constantly lopped by axes. Then cattle and sheep were brought to graze, nibbling the new shoots. Finally Ox Mountain became bald. If a person is repeatedly in situations not conducive to virtuous behavior, over a period of time the effect on benevolence will be comparable.

We have already seen that Mencius's view allows for the possibility that many people will have a strong motivation of benevolence only occasionally. Habits of not thinking of other people's well-being can make the incidence of such motivations dwindle. Insensitivity—not really taking in the other's pain—can facilitate this process. Behind all of this is the fact, in Mencius's view, that the great majority of people, even when their conduct is reasonably virtuous, do not really understand what they are doing (book 7, A.5). Their behavior is guided more, then, by habits and the vagaries of what gets their attention than by any overarching vision.

Extending Benevolence

Thus far we have seen how Mencius argues for his thesis that benevolence is innate, and how he defends it against the obvious objections that are based on examples of behavior that fails in benevolence and the occasional cases of people who are totally lacking in it. If the goal of Mencius's philosophy had been merely to create a sound moral psychology, he might well have thought that this set of arguments largely completed his project. Like most classical Chinese philosophers, though, he has larger social and moral goals, including an educational role in leading people toward a good society. In terms of this larger goal, the crucial question becomes "How can people who display flashes of benevolence be led to express their inner benevolence consistently and effectively?"

This is the project of *extending* benevolence. It has a component of the philosophical analysis that is characteristic of moral psychology, seeking to understand the difference between being occasionally benevolent and being thoroughly benevolent. But Mencius sees it also as a project of the greatest ethical and political importance.

The issues are extremely complicated and difficult, and it would be wrong to see Mencius as having a clearly developed set of solutions. He has a number of ideas, some more ingenious than others. At moments he wants to say, in the words of a recent commercial for sneakers, "Just do it." Someone who occasionally displays benevolence surely can *will* that this be more consistent.

Maybe not. People who go on diets often are capable, on any given occasion, of turning down tempting food, but find it extremely difficult to do this on every single occasion. Similarly, it may be that many people can rise to an occasion by doing something virtuous but would find it far more difficult to be consistently and thoroughly virtuous.

It may help the king who spared the ox if he is made more mindful of the peasants whom he does not see who are near starvation. Encouragement to extend benevolence also can build on making him more mindful of the traces of benevolence in his nature. Thus even fondness for music can be connected with benevolence (book 1, B.1), in that people naturally wish to share with others the music that they like.

At other moments Mencius seems keenly aware that extending benevolence is not simply a matter of willpower. Benevolence, he observes (book 4, A.19), needs to be ripe. What ripeness is must be seen in terms of personal refinement, about which Mencius (as we will see) has a good deal to say. Stages of personal refinement cannot be simply willed, nor can they be rushed. Mencius jokes about this in a story (book 2, A.2) about a farmer who was so anxious for his plants to grow that he pulled at them. He then went home, telling his family that he was worn out from helping the plants to grow; but they found the plants uprooted and dead.

The gradual process of refinement is crucial. But so is a broadened sense of what systematic benevolence is concerned with. Ethics that is taught to large groups of people, which includes the ethics of the Ten Commandments, will naturally have as a major concern the requirements of order and personal security in a viable society. It will consist predominantly of prohibitions, "Thou shalt not"s. Both Confucius and Mencius would agree that these elements of ethics are very important. But perhaps there is a case for including also a larger number of "Thou shalt"s.

One of the difficulties is that it is often easier to formulate for general consumption what you shouldn't do than what you should do. Nevertheless, it clearly makes sense to think of genuine benevolence as focusing at least as much on what you should do for people as on what you shouldn't do to them. Our normal sense of what virtue is—in the light of the guidelines we were handed as children—centers on things (e.g., torture, brutality, etc.) that a virtuous person simply will not do. But in Mencius's view a really benevolent person should extend what one will not do to what one *will* do (book 7, B.31). We need to move, in other words, from our set of absolute inhibitions outward to positive acts to benefit people.

It is often much harder to see what will benefit people than it is to see what will harm them. To extend our benevolence to positive behavior requires more mindfulness and thought. Being truly virtuous, Mencius remarks (book 7, B.10), requires ongoing alertness, like business success. Reflection on other people's psychology and on how the world works will be part of this process.

Refinement

In Mencius's view, as in Confucius's, both ritual and music play crucial roles in the process of refinement. Ritual is especially important in the gentleman's retaining his heart, by which I think Mencius means (among other things) his innate benevolence. The courtesy it embodies expresses respect for others (book 4, B.28). The right sort of music—what Mencius calls "benevolent music" (book 7, A.14)—can have a profound influence, presumably in harmonizing and deepening one's structure of emotions.

Refinement also requires continuous self-monitoring, which will include bouts of self-criticism. Some of these will be provoked by other people's responses. Hume, in book 2 of his *Treatise of Human Nature,* speaks of the important role of "mirroring fellow minds" in the formation of self. Mencius also is concerned with mirroring fellow minds, but especially when the images they provide are not those one hoped for.

If others do not respond to your benevolence, you must look inside yourself (book 4, A.4.). Perhaps there has been a problem in communication. But there is a deeper and more disturbing possibility: that one's "goodness" is more self-absorbed and self-aggrandizing than one would like to think. Mencius cautions against trying to dominate people through goodness (book 4, B.16). What feels like virtue may have as one of its sides an attempt to make other people feel indebted or respectful. If people often do not respond well to this, we might take it as a useful warning sign. For that matter, shame, Mencius insists (book 7, A.6 and 7), is very useful in personal growth.

Becoming a really good person, in Mencius's view, should be a preoccupation, so that one steeps oneself in the ideal of life as it should be lived (book 4, B.14). Thinking about this way of life will involve a multiplicity of concerns. Detail really matters to someone who is refining a personal style and trying to be effectively benevolent. But there is also an essential nature at the root of refinement, so that it is important also to maintain the connection with innate benevolence and in at least this sense to retain one's child's heart.

Fulfillment

Some of what Mencius has to say about the rewards of thoroughgoing and wholehearted benevolence is somewhat surprising. As a Confucian, he of course emphasizes the degree to which personal refinement creates a degree of invulnerability, in that much of what one values (including one's own psychological harmony) is not subject to chance. If vexations do arise (book 4, B.28), the gentleman, thanks to inner resources, will not be perturbed.

What is surprising is the discourse of the visible manifestations of thorough benevolence that runs through Mencius. The benevolence of a gentleman who follows it as his nature—who we might say really gets into it—is visible in his face and shows in his back and limbs (book 7, A.21). This is a Confucian counterpart of the Zen insistence (see chapter 8) that spiritual development is apparent (to those who know how to see) in bodily deportment and movement.

There also is increased energy. Part of this energy stems from the poise that is possible for someone who has found out who she or he is, and is at one with that identity. Mencius himself remarks that his heart has not stirred since he was 40. Perhaps most of us are short of energy because we lack this kind of poise, or because much of the time we are uncertain about what we are doing. The operative Chinese concept here is *qi (ch'i),* which means spirit or vital energy. Mencius, who usually is reasonably modest about what he has attained, speaks in book 2, A.2 of his floodlike *qi.* The earlier work on the mindfulness and single-mindedness required for thorough benevolence has as one of its rewards an ongoing sense of vitality.

Mencius's image of fulfillment, in short, goes far beyond a record of good conduct. It is an image of a psychological system that is liberated from conflict by its wholehearted adherence to its innate benevolence, and that in the process is energized. The goodness that this liberated system will represent will be evident, to those who are perceptive, in demeanor and in nuances of style. The ethics that this system represents is so different from what most of us would regard as traditional that it deserves further comment. The ethics can be appreciated in terms of the contrast between the truly good person, on one hand, and, on the other hand, someone that Mencius (and before him Confucius) considered a bad imitation of real virtue, "the honest villager," whom Confucius denounced as the enemy of virtue.

Mencius repeats this condemnation (book 7, B.37), in the process diagnosing the honest villager's problem as inordinate desire for other people's approval. His perceptive comment about a man whose desire to be seen as virtuous exceeds his desire to be virtuous is that "If you want to censure him, you can't find anything" (D. C. Lau's translation).

At first this may seem puzzling. If there genuinely is nothing for which you can criticize the honest villager, then why not respect him? He sounds perfect. The answer lies in a difference between the ethical standards that Mencius shares with Confucius and those by which the great majority of people judge. The ethics of Confucius, as indicated in the previous chapter, is one of nuance: what matters is not only the *kind* of thing that is done, but also the way in which it was done and the spirit in which it is done. Inner attitudes matter and will be seen by those who know how to look. If you do the generous thing not from a benevolent motive but from a desire for good reputation, this will show in your face (book 7, B.11).

The average person (in the Confucian view) does not always see all of this clearly and also tends to be insensitive to nuances. Hence the standards of goodness for general use are likely to consist of rules of propriety. Many of us have known people who are very adroit at staying on the right side of such rules, but who aren't exactly kind or benevolent; in fact, they really aren't nice people, but they always manage to be in the "right." Mencius regards such people as not genuinely good. Their deficiencies can become more generally apparent when they are confronted with cases that are hard to judge by means merely of traditional categories, or when dominant social influences change. Even if this never happens, and they successfully pass as "good," their lives will lack the systemic rewards that go along with genuine goodness.

Conclusion

Mencius holds a view of genuine goodness that is not at all far from Confucius's. Real goodness goes far beyond meaning well, and indeed well beyond the "virtue" of the average upstanding citizen. To be truly virtuous is to be reliably good in one's behavior, even in difficult circumstances or in cases that are difficult to judge. This requires the ability to determine what is appropriate in unusual and complicated circumstances. True virtue in this respect presupposes reflection on experience and an openness to nonstandard solutions. It also requires valuing itself: the truly virtuous person will, whatever comes, find some satisfaction in the personality structure of being virtuous.

Because of all of this, Mencius, like Confucius, believes that true goodness should be seen as built on a long process of refinement, in which ritual and music play major parts; and the process is never entirely finished. There are two major respects, though, in which Mencius goes well beyond anything in *The Analects of Confucius*. One is that Mencius links goodness with personal energy. The psychic harmony that true virtue requires can be seen as the opposite of neurosis, and one of its marks is heightened energy.

The other novel element in Mencius is that he argues that benevolence is an innate element in human nature. He anticipates plausible objections and provides reasons for not regarding them as crippling. Given this thesis, he sees the central problem in ethics to be the gap between the flickering manifestations in most people of innate benevolence, on one hand, and consistent, intelligent benevolent behavior, on the other.

Recommended Reading

Kwong-loi Shun, *Mencius and Early Chinese Thought* (Stanford: Stanford University Press, 1997) is a magisterial study—both philosophically sharp and very thorough—of Mencius.

David S. Nivison, *Ways of Confucianism,* ed. Bryan Van Norden (LaSalle: Open Court, 1997), includes some very penetrating examinations of Mencius's moral psychology, and also discussion of the third century BCE. Confucian philosopher Xunzi, whom many saw as diametrically opposed to Mencius's view of human nature.

Angus C. Graham, "The Background of the Mencian Theory of Human Nature," in A. C. Graham, *Studies in Chinese Philosophy and Philosophical Literature* (New York: State University of New York Press, 7–66). This is a much admired account of the intellectual context of Mencius's thought, given by a great scholar and translator of Chinese philosophy.

I. A. Richards's *Mencius on the Mind* (London: Kegan Paul, Trench & Trubner, 1932). This is an interesting attempt to relate Mencius to issues in twentieth-century thought.

Martin L. Hoffman, "Interaction of Affect and Cognition in Empathy," in *Emotions, Cognition, and Behavior,* ed. Carroll E. Izard, Jerome Kagan, and Robert B. Zajonc (Cambridge: Cambridge University Press, 1984), pp. 103–31. This presents evidence for empathy of response, of a sort that might well be connected with benevolence, in very young children.

SIX

DAODEJING (TAO TE CHING)

In this chapter we enter the world of Daoism (Taoism), the great rival of Confucianism in ancient China. Of the two, Daoism is the more colorful. It has captured Western imaginations: witness books ranging from the *Tao of Pooh* to the *Tao of Physics*. Its original advocates clearly were eccentric people, and there is a mysticism that makes readers think that they are being given access to deep truths. But it is not so easy to say what these deep truths are supposed to be.

According to legend the eighty one poems that compose the Daodejing (also known in the older romanization as Tao Te Ching) are the work of Lao Tzu, a contemporary of Confucius in the sixth century BCE. He has been thought of as the great founder of Daoism. Was there a real Lao Tzu? It may be that the original inspiration of the Daodejing was at the time of Confucius, or even before. But scholars now agree that the work we actually have dates from about two hundred years or more after then.

Were there Daoists as early as the time of Confucius? I have not yet said what Daoism is, or explored what it is to be a Daoist. But the reader will see that one of the typical characteristics of Daoists is that they avoid attention. Hence it would be too much to expect that there would be early historical records of Daoists.

Characters who sound like Daoists do appear in *The Analects of Confucius* (book 14, 41; book 18, 5–7). Confucius tries to talk with some of them, and they avoid him. Even though these passages themselves may date from a somewhat later time than the rest of the

Analects, they do suggest that there were Daoists in a very early period, long before classic Daoist texts like the Daodeching took their final form.

Daoism

The term "Daoism," like Western terms (such as "existentialism" or "empiricism") for philosophical movements or schools of thought, groups together thinkers and texts that are not entirely the same. The great Daoist text the Zhuangzi (Chuang-Tzu) that is the subject of the next chapter is in some ways very different from the Daodejing. They share some things, including a distrust of literal readings of what the world is like and a contempt for moral earnestness. Both offer an ethics that points toward lives that will be emotionally freer and less "respectable" than those endorsed by Confucianism.

The central concept of Daoism is the *dao* (*tao*). This is normally translated as "way" or "path." The term "dao" is available, much like terms such as "democracy" and "freedom," to people who have widely divergent views of what they are talking about. Confucius repeatedly speaks about his version of the *dao,* the way of life for a Confucian worthy that should become so ingrained that it is no longer a matter of choice.

The *dao* of Daoism is very different from this. Typically a major element in the *dao* of Daoism is a harmony with the natural world, which includes the primitive emotional structures of humanity. To follow this *dao* is never actively to go against the rhythms of the world, and never to undergo a tense struggle with your own emotions or desires.

To be a Daoist, then, is to be very much at home in the natural world. In a quiet, inconspicuous way one may steer the course of events. But Daoists do not strive actively to change things, and on the whole their relationship with the course of nature is passive and re-sponsive rather than active. Clearly the calm that a Daoist is supposed to have will be the result of a long history of controlled self-shaping. But again, this self-control will be a matter of a gradual process of shaping and steering one's emotions and inclinations. There will be no struggles, and no confrontations—either within oneself or with the world outside of oneself.

Some of these elements are emphasized in the Daodejing, which especially dwells on our littleness in relation to the cosmic forces of nature. This sense of relative importance connects with, and undoubtedly contributed to, a marked element of traditional Chinese culture. It is expressed in those classic landscapes in which tiny human figures can be discerned amidst spectacular scenes of mountains and water.

The Daodejing also emphasizes the importance of passivity. Traditional Chinese society, with its preoccupation with politeness and ceremonial correctness, along with the growing moral seriousness of Confucianism, was extremely patriarchal. So it may surprise the reader that the Daodejing equates the skilled passivity it recommends with the feminine. But then Daoism has to be seen as a counterculture, rather than as representing the dominant tendencies of the culture.

It may be that any philosophy that is rich and interesting has its points of tension, elements of the philosophy that are not easy to fit together. One such point in Confucianism occurs at the intersection between the insistence that the Confucian worthy will have peace of mind (because the things he most values are within himself and therefore within his control), and the insistence that the Confucian worthy should make a strong effort to strengthen goodness in the society (and that the effort might well fail in a galling way). Daoism emphasizes a kind of natural ease in life, in which one's harmony with the world leads to lack of struggle, confrontation, and risk. At the same time there is a rueful recognition that, from the Daoist point of view, there is something positively unnatural about contemporary societies, given their obsession with ritual politeness and with moral standards. Thus there is a tension point. To be in harmony with nature and with the basic structures of human emotions may lead to being out of harmony with society. The Daoist might be seen as a social misfit, with some unsettling results.

There can be strategies to mitigate the tensions inherent in a philosophy, even if they cannot be eliminated. The obvious thought for a Daoist is that conflicts with the surrounding society can be eased in a number of ways. Most dramatically, one can simply leave the social centers and retreat into the countryside. Some of the Daoist-sounding characters reported in the *Analects* are encountered in what sound like remote rural areas and might have been mistaken for ordinary peasants.

Another strategy is to "drop out," to become someone who will not be taken seriously or will be ignored. This goal could be accomplished by acting crazy. Witness the strategy of the "madman of Ch'u" (*Analects* 18, 5), who in a sharp, coherent way points out to Confucius that his do-gooder way of life is dangerous and futile but then refuses to speak further with Confucius, and plainly is carrying on the role of local madman.

A more complicated strategy, which may have been more possible later than it was in the early period, would be to separate a domain of private and secluded life (perhaps with friends and family) from that of the public and ceremonial world, and to give Daoist tendencies free rein in time spent in private. Someone who pursued this kind of strategy could be in some respects a Confucian and in some respects a Daoist. But it would be oversimple to suppose that tendencies from one area of life would never seep into the other.

Mysticism in the Daodejing

There are a number of good translations of the Daodejing. Quotations in what follows generally will be from R. B. Blakney's translation, *The Way of Life* (Mentor Books), the poetical qualities of which seem to me to be felicitous. There will be occasional comparisons to other translations.

The first poem in the traditional ordering sets the tone for a philosophy allied to mysticism and also introduces a countercultural feminism. "There are ways but the Way is uncharted," the poem begins; Stephen Aldiss and Stanley Lombardo have "Tao called Tao is not Tao." It is made clear that the subject is a knowledge that cannot adequately be put in words. There is a cosmic order. "Things have a mother and she has a name." The countercultural feminism reappears in poem 6: "The valley spirit is not dead: They say it is the mystic female."

We should say something about mysticism, which is a loose label for a variety of nonstandard patterns of thought and experience that seem to give a deeper-than-normal access to reality. Do the Upanishads count as mystical treatises? They have (as chapter 1 argued) a structure of argument and analysis that in its way seems unmystical. But on the other hand, the thesis that *atman* is Brahman is held to present a deeper-than-normal view of reality, resting on experience that requires special preparation and that is not at all easy to characterize.

The centrality of experience of an unusual kind that is difficult to report in any literal way is characteristic of mysticism. Poem 1 of the Daodejing seems to point toward experiences of this sort. It should be reemphasized that not all mysticisms are alike. Whatever experience poem 1 is about clearly differs greatly from those crucial to the Upanishads. Further, to the extent that preparation is required in order to have the experience, it will be preparation of a different sort. Also, the difficulty of reporting the nature of the experience should not be viewed in oversimple terms. Mystics, after all, sometimes write books. They are not tongue-tied. Clearly part of the problem is that available vocabulary falls along the lines of common experiences, so that any experience of an uncommon quality cannot be communicated without distortion in familiar terms. This difficulty is not unique to mysticism. It is often observed that there is a similar difficulty in communicating emotional experiences of a rich and subtle nature. The verbal infrastructure required for literal renderings is simply not available. So the experiences must be communicated, if at all, in a nonliteral medium, such as poetry.

Hence there is a natural affinity between mystical experience and poetical expression. But there are also nonpoetical techniques of expression. The Upanishads tend to be nonpoetical in style, perhaps because the central experience of *atman* is so far removed from the chart of normal experience. The normal stretch of poetical or metaphoric language hardly extends so far. The fallback strategy is, then, a combination of negatives (the experience of *atman* is not at all like normal awakeness or dreaming) with a guarded comparison (the state of being in touch with *atman* is less unlike dreamless sleep).

Something like this fallback strategy is evident in some of the Western philosophical literature about God. Philosophers like Maimonides and St. Thomas Aquinas insist that the understanding of God of which we are capable is principally negative. God's qualities are not the limited qualities with which we are familiar. We can describe God by saying what God is not. (God is not limited in power, knowledge, or goodness, etc.)

The poems of the Daodajing make their mystical point mainly by speaking of a "form without form" (poem 35), or stressing the elusiveness of what is important and the dreamlike character of one's sense of it. It also is very clear that the Way is hardly an object of detached contemplation. To know the *dao*, that is, is knowledge that cannot be analyzed in terms of the formation of correct sentences. Rather it is knowledge of how to live: it is "knowing how" rather than "knowing that."

At least two of the translations of the poem traditionally numbered 1 bring out the active, practical nature of the knowledge in question, and also that what is recommended is an ideal rather than something fully attainable. Victor Mair (Bantam Books), for whom this is poem

45, has "The ways that can be walked are not the eternal Way." James Legge's translation (originally in the Oxford Sacred Books of the East series as *Texts of Taoism*, 1891) has "The Tao that can be trodden is not the enduring and unchanging Tao."

What is presented is a mysticism of being able to live in a certain kind of way. Many of the poems make it clear that the recommended style of life involves freedom rather than rule following and has strong links to the emotions. So of course it cannot be reduced to a formula or formulas, but also it cannot be expected to be finely polished and perfect.

The Argument

Earlier in this book I suggested that a major characteristic of philosophy is that it has arguments for its positions. The argument may be explicit or implicit. If the Daodejing is philosophy, then one would expect a structure of argument. The poems, however, on the face of them, do not look like patterns of reasoning. There are no obvious arrangements of premises and conclusions.

Nevertheless, the Daodejing can be read as philosophy. Here are two claims that run through much of it, and that are supported by an implicit structure of argument. As so often is the case in Asian philosophy, the argument appeals at least in part to experience that one has had or might have.

> Claim 1. It is possible to become sensitive to a dynamic in events in the world (that is, to the tendency of things to develop in a certain way).
>
> Claim 2. It is more satisfying and productive to adapt to this dynamic than to go counter to it.

Together these claims point toward a life strategy of passivity and responsiveness, which (in a bit of gender stereotyping) are spoken of as expressing one's feminine side.

Claim 2 is a straightforward ethical claim about the competing values of various styles of life. The argument for it has to be experiential, in a broad sense that includes appeals to actual experience and observation and also to an imagined grasp of what it is like to pursue various styles of life. You can experience what it is like to adapt to events, not to struggle, and to feel both relaxed and in command of what you are doing; or you may observe people for whom this appears true (and who seem to enjoy their lives); or you can imaginatively construct some sense of what it would be like. Once you experience such a life, or have some sense of what it is like, you become aware that it is much nicer than the kind of life that the great majority of people lead. (The way in which such experience or imaginative reconstuction can be linked to knowledge is explored in my *Value . . . and What Follows*, Oxford University Press, 1999.)

The argument for claim 1 has to be experiential in a different way. In the abstract, it might seem entirely possible that the world is blindly chaotic. If that were so, then the attempts (which Daoists decry) drastically to change the world would be futile, but on the other hand, Daoist strategies wouldn't do any better. If claim 1 is correct, then, it must be possible to experience an inherent tendency of development in some courses of events.

Given the complexity of historical processes, we may assume that such an inner dynamic would be unlikely to be captured adequately in formulas. Some formulas (such as "You can't change the world" or "People often will resist attempts to make them perfect") will have their uses. But a fine-grained and advanced knowledge here would be, in large part, a matter of shrewd intuitions, tempered by continued monitoring.

Indeed, the Daoist conception of real knowledge looks like an inversion of Plato's. Plato, writing in Greece more than a century after the legendary Lao Tzu, insisted that true knowledge is of the unchanging (Being) and never of the changing (Becoming). In effect, the experiences to which the Daodejing appeals point toward the opposite view.

Despite the intuitive, hard-to-formulate, nature of most knowledge of how things are developing, the Daodejing does suggest that there are some recurring patterns. One is a kind of psychic-social counterpart to Sir Isaac Newton's law that every action has an equal and opposite reaction. Something like this is held to be true in the social and political sphere.

Lao Tzu's Law: The consequences of pushing for something often will include elements that amount to the opposite of what is pushed for.

Poem 18 (in the traditional numbering) is a locus classicus for this line of thought. It charts a decline from an earlier primitive simplicity. When the way declines, an immediate symptom is the appearance of kindness and morality. Even worse, wisdom and intelligence appear, producing hypocrisy. As the natural harmony of society is lost, codes are introduced to maintain order. At the low point, when the social and political fabric has lost its strength, "official loyalty" (Stephen Mitchell's translation for Harper & Row has "patriotism") becomes the style.

A curious feature of this capsule history of the world thus far is that it reverses the model of the nineteenth-century German philosopher Hegel. (Karl Marx, who came after Hegel, claimed to turn him on his head, but the Daodejing merely sends him into reverse.) Hegel's model is that the progress of history occurs in the form of a development (thesis) provoking its opposite (antithesis), this ultimately leading to an outcome that combines features or elements of both (synthesis). Hegel thought of theses as developments in ideas; Marx thought of socioeconomic results of changes in the mode of production. The Daodejing's model is that a primitive unity, which might be thought of as like a synthesis, breaks up, and resolves itself into thesis and antithesis.

What is most striking in this Daoist model is the contention that virtues have produced vices. This line of thought will seem so counterintuitive to so many people that it requires considerable explanation. The main assumption is that the virtues (and also conspicuous achievements) amount to pushes against the world. Besides this, they in effect proclaim standards, thus dividing people and their performances into those that meet the standards and those that do not.

On the face of it, virtues and conspicuous achievements push the world in a positive direction. Not only do they directly contribute something positive, but also they can be emulated by others, thus leading to other positive contributions. Part of the Daoist thought, though, is that, alongside these positive consequences (which presumably are intended), there will be other consequences that are unintended and may be not at all positive. In this one respect Daoist thought runs parallel to one element, associated with Friedrich A. von Hayek, in modern conservativism: the idea that social changes in general have unintended consequences, so that what looks like positive social engineering can turn out to have mixed or negative results. (This is a limited similarity; there is no reason to think that Hayek would like most of what is in Daoism, or that Daoists would like most of what is in Hayek.)

Here is what I think is the Daodejing's view of the appearance of virtues (and conspicuous achievements) and of their unintended consequences. First, it is often observed that virtues (that is, not merely the notion of the virtues but their actual practice *as* virtues) presuppose a social world in which whatever the virtue represents cannot be counted on. Immanuel Kant observed that "holy" beings would not have a morality. That is, they could not generate the idea of it, because what it recommends will be taken as a matter of course; and hence their good behavior would not be *moral* good behavior. In a primitive society in which community values are integral, natural behavior should not create any serious problems (or so Daoists believe). Hence morality would not appear. The appearance of morality thus is a sign that the community is falling apart.

The development and articulation of virtues creates, as poem 2 points out, logical room for the corresponding vices. Once we create the idea of beauty, there is ugliness. Goodness gives us wickedness. Conspicuous achievement also gives us the now highly visible category of failure. Real achievements will coexist with real failures. Together, virtues and conspicuous achievements polarize the world.

There is a mixture here of logical and empirical points. Perhaps the polarization can be seen as a two-step process. First there is creation of a category, including a notion of something as required or as praiseworthy, which entails the complementary notion of something else as unacceptable or as falling short. This much is logic. The philosopher Gilbert Ryle once pointed out that there could not be counterfeit coins in the world unless there were (or at least had been?) real ones. But a similar logic tells us that we cannot think of coins as real without allowing for the possibility of counterfeit ones.

In some cases, once standards are established that separate what is acceptable or praiseworthy from what is not, it is inevitable that some people or things fall short. In these cases, it could be argued that creation of the standards did not cause the poor performances, but at most caused us to view the inevitable poor performances in a certain way. To say merely this, though, overlooks the further dynamics of inadequacy and failure. Those who fall short may then try harder, but in some circumstances it is at least as likely that they will simply give up or become "oppositional."

We have to expect some perverse responses. People often react against standards that seem designed to yield negative judgments about them. Further, being "bad" can seem more exciting than being barely adequate. It is not thrilling to be told that you are harmless.

There may be some inherent human contrariety above and beyond this. If you want to bring it about that some children push carrots up their noses, one way is to tell large numbers of them that on no account are they to do this. If a desired outcome is that numbers of college freshmen drink to the point of being sick to their stomachs, the likelihood might be increased by changing the law so that they are too young to drink legally at all.

It should be stressed that what I termed Lao Tzu's Law is, of course, not really like a law of physics, and that in particular the operative word is "often." Indeed, Daoists reject formulaic approaches to the world, even those whose formulas mimic Daoism. Thus it would be simple-minded and un-Daoist to suppose that making something illegal or strongly recommending against it *always* produces some contrary responses. A lot may depend on how the recommendation or prohibition is handled, as well as the kind of thing that is interdicted. The most basic point is that the course of events cannot be appreciated in terms of invariable patterns or formulas. Sensitive monitoring and some flexibility of interpretation are required.

Nevertheless, poem 18 and also poem 38 make clear that there has been a recurring pattern of breakdowns in common values, and that this led to recognition of virtues, which has led in turn to more conspicuous practice of vices. Arguably this is not intended as the whole story of human history, and I will argue that it certainly is not intended as a template for future history. The actual course of events always will be more complex and subtle than any simple generalization can indicate. The recurring pattern of breakdowns that is noted will merely give a clue as to a useful way to approach *many* patterns of events.

Let me sum up the discussion thus far of claim 1. The claim is that there is a dynamic in events to which one can be sensitive. The main argument for this rests on the experience of people (who may include skilled politicians and social observers, and also people who pick up quickly on trouble signs in the personal relations that matter to them) who do seem to have a sense of the ways in which events are developing. Often, developing situations will have to be "played by ear." But there are some loose generalizations that can be known about in advance. These include that pushing at the world usually does not work, and that conspicuous positive efforts often have unintended negative consequences. Altogether this adds up, at least in my view, to an argument of some strength for claim 1.

Claim 2 recommends adapting to the dynamic of events. I have already suggested that the argument for claim 2 appeals to experience of what the life it recommends is like (and of what its value seems to be). This may be one's own personal experience, or can be keyed to a sense of what the lives are like of people who approximate the ideal. Either way, experience shows (in the Daoist view) that a life of Daoist adaptation to the dynamic of events is much more gratifying than other kinds of lives.

Passivity, Responsiveness

We need, however, to become clearer about what is recommended. What the Daodejing endorses is not easy to grasp, and certainly is far more complicated and nuanced than any brief phrase can convey. Adapting to the dynamic of events can be, for example, in some cases a far cry from collaborating with it.

It would be wrong to read claim 2 as a recommendation of conformity. Perhaps the frequent approving reference to the "feminine" should be taken more seriously than it usually is? It is only in some outlandish male fantasy worlds that "feminine" means "compliant." Perhaps the approval of the "feminine" in the Daodejing points toward ways of maintaining independent action while avoiding direct confrontation?

Poem 15 describes great Daoist masters of the past, who were careful and alert (Mitchell)/cautious and watchful (Blakney), and also receptive. The passivity and receptiveness that the Daodejing recommends clearly should not be confused with, as it were, closing your eyes and letting events sweep over you. Many readers can be misled, not only by simplistic stereotypes about what the "feminine" is supposed to entail, but also by simplistic stereotypes about mysticism. Some will associate mysticism with trances or with a vagueness that extends from language to behavior. So one might have an image of the good Daoist as locked in a mysterious inner world, or as soft and compliant in everything said or done. All of this is wrong. Poem 15 especially makes clear that Daoist responsiveness is hardly trancelike, that it requires heightened alertness rather than vagueness of mind, and that its "feminine" nature is very different from being carried along by the course of events.

It is true that, in the Daoist view of things, the wise man is self-effacing (poem 15) and does not tinker or tamper with the world (poem 29). Poem 76 recommends against rigor and being stiff, and praises what is supple and soft. The Daoist idea of responsiveness does include avoidance of direct confrontations, or oppositions in which there is no room to maneuver.

Daoist responsiveness is best approached, as it were, from the inside outward, by first examining the recommended emotional modifications. In this matter Daoism can be compared to a Western philosophy that centers on the idea of a world that we cannot control, namely stoicism. There are some obvious parallels. Neither Daoism nor stoicism recommends that we struggle to master the world. Both recommend emotional modifications so that we do not suffer from anger, resentment, or frustration at the uncontrollable nature of the world.

The Way, according to poem 48 (Blakney), is "gained by daily loss." (Mair, for whom this is poem 11, has "daily decrease.") This loss is not merely of emotions (or of intensity of emotion). It includes the falling away of formulaic judgments of the world and of automatic responses. Both the Daodejing and the other great Daoist text, the Zhuangzi, are permeated with contempt for people who approach the world through generalizations and insist on sharp dividing lines. If the good Daoist is cautious and watchful, then automatic responses (which are allied to unconsciousness or semiconsciousness of the details of what is going on) are to be discouraged.

Daily emotional loss can be linked with the recurrent praise in the Daodejing for emptiness and for stillness. Emptiness should not be confused with vacuity, or with affectlessness. Clearly life as a Daoist is meant to be enjoyable. There is affect. Instead, the emptiness that is extolled has a lot in common with what we would normally term "openness." To give up on formulas and on automatic responses is to take things as they come, without preconceptions. The stillness has a lot to do with what happens (or does not happen) when the skilled athlete, actor, musician, or conversationalist waits to see what the best next move is. It denotes poise, and a refusal to fill the time with false moves or emotions.

A plausible reconstruction of the emotional landscape of Daoism is that emotions of all kinds are meant to be less strong and pressing. Their force will dwindle, but that does not mean that they are supposed to disappear. The watchful, cautious Daoist will tend to avoid quick emotional responses. Someone who is mindful of the dynamic of the world, also, will be most unlikely to have emotions of anger, resentment, or for that matter fear. These emotions are entirely unproductive. You often can manage to sidestep the kinds of things that might inspire anger or resentment or give rise to fear. The emotions themselves usually do not contribute to the responsiveness that this requires, and in fact can interfere with the process of taking in the details of a difficult situation.

Let us return to the comparison of Daoism with stoicism. Both are rich, complex philosophies, represented by more than one major text, so that general and precise-sounding comparisons are apt to be misleading. Nevertheless, it is clear that Daoism and stoicism have different general *tendencies* in their recommended responses to the uncontrollable nature of the world. It seems to me that stoicism more often leans toward an inner withdrawal from the frustrating world. Despite its mystical passages, the Daodejing does not lean at all toward such an inner withdrawal. One continues to look at the world, through hooded eyes; and the focus is not merely on the dynamics of the world, but also on what one is to do.

A striking, very specific element in this is breath contol. This emerges toward the beginning of poem 10. Disciplined knowledge of how to breathe is held to be important to spiritual advancement. It also was thought to contribute to longevity. (This idea gained prominence as Daoism evolved from a countercultural movement and philosophy into an organized religion with a penumbra of magical and alchemical secrets for long life.) Breath control of course is ongoing. Like most of what Daoist texts recommend, it is not a matter of a momentary choice but rather is meant to be an element in a long-term stance. Central to the ideal relation to the world is a calm steadiness, which contributes to a poised ability to deal with whatever comes.

The passivity of Daoism, in short, is of the wait-and-see variety. It most certainly does *not* imply that one will become the slavish follower of whatever totalitarian leader appears on the scene, or that one will be caught up in the latest fad. Indeed, the Daodejing cannot be appreciated unless we realize that the continuous assumption is that a good Daoist is, and will continue to be, an independent agent and not a conformist or a doormat.

This means that what the Daoist does makes a difference, at least to the Daoist herself or himself (and, insofar as the Daoist is part of the world, to the world). How can this be? We know that the Daodejing regards pushing at the world as futile and counterproductive, and that it recommends against tinkering with the world. Can we make sense of a passivity that is in some respects active?

The relevant concept in the Daodejing is *wu wei*, which is generally translated as "doing nothing." As always, though, we have to be open to the possibility that what is meant is more subtle and qualified than the simplest and most direct translation might indicate. When someone asks "What are you doing?" and you answer "Nothing," this may mean that you were doing nothing special, or nothing out of the ordinary, or nothing that stands out. Only rarely does it mean that you are stock still. (And indeed, to be stock still is fairly unusual and *would* stand out.) An alternative translation of "wu wei" as activity that does not disrupt the way of heaven/nature is less misleading.

The Dynamics of Social Change

In order to explore further the nature of Daoist passivity, we need also to take up a difficult issue of interpretation. Many of the poems of the Daodejing are concerned with statecraft, and in particular with how a wise ruler will manage a country. If we start with the image of Daoism as concerned with what is mystical, involving a withdrawal from the social concerns that were so prominent among Confucians, these poems will seem odd and discordant in relation to the rest of the work. An obvious thought is that perhaps they indeed do not fit. They could be regarded as having been added on at some later date to a work-in-progress that was mystical and apolitical.

The interpretation of the political poems as add-ons might gain plausibility if we accept that the composition of the Daodejing in its present form occurred over a considerable period. During this period, China was divided into a number of kingdoms, many of whose rulers hoped to be the one who would conquer the others and reestablish an empire. Quite possibly most of these rulers did not have a clue as to what would work, and therefore were willing to listen to traveling philosophers who gave advice on statecraft. Mencius was one such traveling philosopher. Perhaps, then, one or more traveling philosophers with some Daoist affinities added his (or their) thoughts to the originally apolitical Daodejing?

At present there is no entirely assured way to answer this question. I would like to suggest, though, that the political poems are not as discontinuous from the rest of the Daodejing as someone who begins with the image of the work as mystical and apolitical might suppose. The first point to make is that, from the point of view of a number of classical Chinese philosophers (including Confucius), the relationship between a ruler and his or her subjects is in a way a personal relationship. This then connects with the point that the activity-within-passivity that seems to be endorsed by the Daodejing extends to personal relationships. Indeed, if a theme of the work is the skill that passivity and responsiveness make possible, then skill in personal relationships would be an important part of the story. The most dramatic example (if there is anything to this interpretation) would be skill as a ruler.

As poem 15 points out, a good Daoist is self-effacing. A recurrent theme in the poems that are concerned with statecraft is that the Daoist ruler does not call attention to himself. Poem 17 recommends that people merely know that he is there, reacting emotionally only to the officials below him. One part of the skill of seeming inactive is, poem 59 suggests, forehandedness. There is a strong contrast between the person who anticipates difficulties and has in place means of dealing with them, on one hand, and the one who lurches from reacting to one crisis to reacting to another. In all spheres of life the Daodejing thinks more highly of the former.

Here we are in a territory of subtle variations in style of behavior that matter a great deal, but are hard (using available language) to indicate with any precision. Daoists are generally contemptuous of people who worry about the future and also are scornful of any preoccupation with the future that causes people to neglect present experience. But it is possible, without worrying or becoming preoccupied, to attain a calm, even awareness of how situations are likely to develop, and to be ready to adjust (again in a calm, even way). This, from the Daoist perspective, is crucial to the management of life. Given proper preparation and a steady stance, one can work, as poem 2 puts it, "by being still." This precludes fiddling and tinkering. Poem 60 compares governing a large country to cooking small fish: too much handling is not a good idea.

All of the strategies for good rulership that are recommended could be employed throughout the spectrum of personal relationships. There can be great advantages in being a steady and still friend, family member, lover, or spouse. Advantages, that is, would accrue to the Daoist in these roles: the relationships would go well. But clearly also someone who manages to apply the spirit of the Daodejing to the spectrum of personal relationships will be relatively easy to get along with, and may be likely to make those connected with her or him feel more relaxed and also better about themselves. It might be hard to analyze what the appeal of such a person was. On the surface, she or he might appear humdrum and ordinary, while inspiring great affection and loyalty. There are a number of very nice dramatizations of this in the Daoist *Zuangzi*, in which the personal merges into the political. One story line is that a ruler has a strong immediate reaction to the personal qualities of someone who in most respects appears quite ordinary, and wishes to make him a high official. The most dramatic instance is Ai T'ai-t'o (in chapter 5), who is exceedingly ugly and never takes the lead in anything; but people are inexplicably attracted to him, and important people trust him. He magnetizes those who come in contact with him.

We are talking about ways in which someone (a ruler, a friend, etc.) can adopt a stance that is designed to have a certain influence. In the case of the ruler, the influence is not only on the relationship between the ruler and subject but also concerns the direction to be taken by the entire polity. This is a way of changing the world. Can this advice (so prominent especially in the poems on statecraft) be reconciled with the admonition that trying to change the world is generally counterproductive?

The answer surely is that there is trying and then there is *trying*, just as there is the kind of activity involved in *wu wei* as contrasted with ordinary activity. The former is inconspicuous, extremely low pressure, and crafted so as not to give rise to sharp conflicts. The Daodejing thinks that this requires real skill and emotional discipline. It also thinks that it can work.

Styles of behavior are difficult to talk about in anything like precise language. I have tried to capture what the Daodejing thinks of as crude and counterproductive in most goal oriented activity by speaking of it as "pushing" at the world. The kind of activity that is consistent with *wu wei* might be spoken of as "steering." The important point is that it preserves an independent role for the agent without being conspicuous or giving rise to confrontations.

There is a different worry that needs to be addressed. Often our ways of talking about legal and moral responsibility are treated as embodying the idea that adults generally are entirely autonomous (and therefore entirely responsible for what they do). Autonomy is respected, which might suggest a negative judgment on anything that impinges on other people's autonomy. It should be emphasized that I am talking about something that has its roots in philosophy (especially the ethical philosophy of Immanuel Kant), but that then plays a role (much of it unanticipated and *not* endorsed by philosophers) in popular, unreflective culture.

The emphasis on autonomy can add up to an ideal (which seems attractive to some people and ridiculous to others) of social relationships as connections between entirely independent and autonomous people. This may be seen to require relationships without influence. Someone who is attracted to this ideal may be especially disturbed by the idea of someone, say a ruler or a friend or family member, who consciously influences other people while giving the appearance of not trying to influence. Is this ethically questionable? If someone consciously adopts the disarming style of relationships recommended in the Daodejing, exerting influence without seeming to do it (or seeming to want to do it), is this manipulative?

In my view, this question does not admit of a simple "Yes" or "No" answer. But what I will say tilts toward "No."

My response starts from the claim that the idea of entire autonomy must be regarded as a highly convenient legal and moral fiction. It facilitates much of the freedom that we enjoy in our society. But a realistic look at what might constitute autonomy suggests that, in any plausible construal, it is a matter of degree, rather than the all-or-nothing matter that we might prefer to believe it to be. There are skills of autonomy, which include the ability to think for oneself and also abilities to weigh situations reasonably and to respond in a sustained, effective manner. Some people master these skills better than others do. (A useful treatment of this is to be found in Diana Meyers's *Self, Society, and Personal Choice.*) The way in which an individual, a group, or a gender is treated can encourage or discourage the development of these skills

Further, it is unreasonable not to be influenced on occasion by good friends who are good people. This is part of having an open mind. We are all to some degree suggestible. How else would advertising work, not to mention our suggestible notion of what is good (that according to many ethical philosophers can be influenced by emotive or prescriptive uses of ethical language)? All of this suggests that there rarely is an entirely definite answer to the question "What does so-and-so want?"

Styles of thought and behavior, and also affects, rub off on others. We are influencing each other all of the time. Could someone refuse to participate in this process—refuse, that is, to influence anyone else? It is hard to imagine how this could be accomplished, unless someone literally disappeared; and even then the disappearance might have some influence.

This is not to deny that there are cases of improper influence. If, say, a teacher indoctrinates students in political and social positions the teacher advocates, this is improper and indeed unprofessional, most especially if it tends to diminish students' abilities to think for themselves. It can be improper even if it is not manipulative.

The word "manipulative" is at home in cases in which the influence both is designed to be largely invisible to the person influenced and runs counter to what she or he reasonably would want. In the worst cases someone consciously calculates what will get other people to do what he or she wants. Sometimes, though, the manipulation is unconscious: it is *as if* someone had consciously calculated how to bend people to his or her will.

It is essential to all of these cases that the influencing is surreptitious and could not be construed as part of appropriate performance of the influencer's normal role or job. If a public official tries to influence citizens not to speed on the highway, or not to engage in the risky behavior of persistent tobacco use, this would not normally be termed manipulation. Nor would it be manipulation if someone tried to influence family members in these directions, by such tactics as mentioning statistics of highway deaths or smoking-related deaths.

What of the king or queen, were there one who followed Daoist advice, whose comportment or behavior is designed to influence subtly the course of events without being obvious in this? In some respects this is like what we would consider manipulative behavior: the influencing is in a way surreptitious. On the other hand, we can imagine that in most cases the comportment or behavior is in plain view. It is only that most people will not take in just how it is that it functions. Further, this is all a normal part of the job of politics. Because of the way political systems work, someone who holds high office will thereby have significant influence over other people, and over the course of events, whether she or he wants to or not.

On balance, therefore, I do not think that we could consider the Daoist ruler to be manipulative. What about ordinary personal relationships, say between friends? Here a lot depends on whether the purposes or goals that can be read into the influence of one friend on another are ones that contribute to the friendship (or to the well-being of the friend who is influenced), or whether they merely represent selfish interests of the influencing friend. If, say, the net result is supposed to be that one friend buys something that the other is selling, influence can look like manipulation. If it is that the friend feels better about herself or himself, or is more comfortable with the friendship, that is quite another matter. Is it manipulation if you phone a friend on her or his birthday, or your mother on Mother's Day?

In thinking about both political dealings and personal relationships, we need to move beyond the crazy abstraction of 100 percent autonomy, and also the abstraction of interactions that are utterly without influence. Plainly we make a difference to each other's lives. High officials, simply by their comportment and images, can make a significant difference; and friends and intimates certainly do. Is there any-

DAODEJING (TAO TE CHING)   III

thing wrong, then, in consciously steering these interactions so as to reduce tensions and confrontations? Perhaps if someone did this while pretending to do the opposite, we would think there was an element of dishonesty. But there is no such element in the case of someone who clearly is disarming and nonconfrontational. The Daodejing suggests that this is a good role to play, and that it can be played with some skill.

If a ruler plays this role, and steers the mood and arrangements of a society so that the polarization of "good" and "bad" is reduced considerably, the thought is that the trend that history thus far has had can be reversed. Syntheses have been falling apart into polar opposites, but they can be reconstructed. This holds out the hope that we can return to an integral society, in which members of a community just naturally, without having to think about it, behave in wholesome ways. Such a community, sounding both peaceful and not at all cosmopolitan, is described in poem 80.

Conclusion

The Daodejing is both mystical and political. The mysticism centers on an awe of nature, and a sense that it is important to be in tune with the natural tendencies of the universe. To be aware of the dynamic of events one needs to be sensitive, taking in details and not relying overly much on formulas. The loose formula that pushing at the world usually is counterproductive is, however, intended to be helpful, by encouraging a tendency to look for nonconfrontational ways of handling problems.

The politics of the Daodejing can be appreciated in relation to the idea that the political is personal. The good Daoist ruler will avoid confrontations with subjects and officials, and will not push at the world. But the course of events can be steered by subtle adjustments, so that a great deal can be accomplished inconspicuously. The history of the world thus far, in the view of the Daodejing, has been one of decline from the natural integrity of communities. Virtues and standards of behavior emerged as people could no longer take for granted how others would behave, and these virtues and norms led to vices and failures. The job of the Daoist ruler is to reverse this without seeming to try, to steer the world back in the direction of a primitive harmony.

Recommended Reading

A. C. Graham gives an excellent general account of the Daodejing_ in *Disputers of the Tao* (La Salle, IL: Open Court, 1989), pp. 215–35.

A good recent collection of essays is *Lao Tzu and the Tao Te Ching*, ed. Livia Kohn and Michael LaFargue (Albany: State University of New York Press, 1989).

The history of Daoism involves an odd mixture of elements. The classic philosophical texts examined in this chapter and the next appear to me to be essentially connected with countercultural styles of life. But over time it became natural to connect the mystical elements of the philosophy with specific religious elements of hope and salvation. This led to the development of Daoism as an organized religion. Other elements attached themselves. The recommended style of life, by eliminating stress and risk taking, plausibly could be linked to greater longevity, hyperbolically expressed in terms of immortality. Hence folk theories about medicine, alchemy, and magic became associated with Daoism. The eventual result was the combination of an organized religion with a set of folkways far less sophisticated than the foundational philosophical texts, but that retained connections with them.

Two good books that examine the development of this multifaceted Daoism are Isabelle Robinet, *Taoism: Growth of a Religion,* trans. Phyllis Brooks (Stanford: Stanford University Press, 1997), and Livia Kohn, *Early Chinese Mysticism: Philosophy and Soteriology in the Taoist Tradition* (Princeton: Princeton University Press, 1992).

Over time Daoism came also to enter people's lives in mixtures with elements of folk religions and mythologies. An interesting case study is the great eighth century CE poet Li Bo (Li Po). An excellent biography, which includes translations of some of the poems, is Arthur Waley's *The Poetry and Career of Li Po* (London: Geo. Allen & Unwin, 1950).

SEVEN

THE ZHUANGZI

Zhuangzi, also known as Chuang-tzu, very probably was a real person, who lived in the fourth century BCE. The book to which his name is attached has accretions that stamp it as the work of many hands. Scholars sometimes isolate within the Zhuangzi (Chuang-Tzu) what are called the "Inner Chapters" (chapters 1 through 7), which are viewed as a core early text and also as exceptionally vivid presentations of the point of view of the book.

That point of view may not be entirely evident right away to the first-time reader. The book is fanciful, and there are many digressions and changes of tone. The overall impression may be of someone who is clever and is fooling around. There are works (the eighteenth-century novel *Tristram Shandy* is an example) whose "unity" is their disunity, their lack of discursive integration; and the Zhuangzi may seem to be one of these works.

Nevertheless, I wish to suggest that at least the Inner Chapters are in their way highly integrated, with no words wasted and no line of thought as random as it may look. There is a consistent set of philosophical positions and implicit arguments for these. Read right, the Zhuangzi is real philosophy—although it also is a lot of fun and is a strangely beautiful book.

Metaphysical Anti-Realism

The apparent fooling around starts in the very first paragraph. We are launched into a fable of a huge fish that becomes a huge bird and does incredible things. A cicada and a little dove are reported as finding the story incredible.

So what's the point? For starters, the perspective of the small insect and small bird is simply different from that of the large fish-bird, or from ours for that matter. A more familiar example might be the way in which some things inaudible to us are audible to dogs. More generally, whatever one's take on any reality is, radically different perspectives always will be possible. Will one of them yield The Truth? The Zhuangzi answers the implied question with a question, noting in the second paragraph that the sky looks blue and asking "Is that its real color?"

In fact, a number of points are being made simultaneously. The primary one is that, because alternative perspectives always are possible, it is unreasonable to suppose that there is a final truth about anything. This smacks of the philosophical position known as anti-realism, which will be discussed shortly. But a secondary point is that, because of the range of possible perspectives, some of which might have real merit, it is important to be humble (unlike the cicada and the little dove). It is also desirable to be open-minded: you might learn something from the other points of view. There is another point, which the passage illustrates rather than saying it or implying it. This is that, if there is no final literal truth, then fanciful language can be at least as good at suggesting insights as sober and conventional language is (and perhaps better?).

There is more than one form of anti-realism. Some anti-realists concentrate on claims about what the world is like, denying that any claim can function simply as an entirely adequate mirror of the world. This is known as metaphysical anti-realism. There also are moral anti-realists, who hold a somewhat (although not entirely) similar view of moral claims, often centering on the denial that there are "moral facts."

In my view the Zhuangzi is permeated with metaphysical anti-realism. Its stand on morality is not easy to assess, partly because morality is not much of a topic. The work is full of suggestions to the effect that certain ways of living are more gratifying and better than others, and indeed that many people lead relatively dreary and unsatisfying lives. These suggestions amount to a set of normative or ethical claims, and Zhuangzi does not seem to have any hesitation about treating them as correct or right. But—if moral judgments are a subset of ethical judgments, consisting of the ones treated as warranting social pressure—the ethical claims that are seemingly endorsed by the

Zhuangzi hardly count as moral. There is nothing immoral per se in having a dreary and unsatisfying life.

Indeed, the topic of morality appears in the book largely in negative comments on moral earnestness. It may be that Zhuangzi, like the authors of the Daodejing, thought of morality as a counterproductive push at the world. Advice on how to lead a more harmonious and satisfying life could be acceptable, while normative judgments that carry the urgency and pressure characteristic of morality would be viewed as dangerous.

Metaphysical anti-realism has been associated with a number of prominent late twentieth-century philosophers. The philosopher of science Thomas S. Kuhn is probably the most famous of these. In *The Structure of Scientific Revolutions,* Kuhn argues that competing scientific theories can have different realities or versions of reality that are incommensurable. The suggestion appears to be very like the point of view of the Zhuangzi, namely, that—whatever picture of the world we happen to have—alternative pictures of the world that are very different could be arrived at (and cannot automatically be dismissed).

In a retrospective "Reply to My Critics" (1970), Kuhn denied that he was a "relativist." Relativism is generally taken to deny that any theory, point of view, or opinion is any better than any other. But Kuhn certainly had not been saying that all scientific theories are equally good, nor was he denying that there is scientific progress. Presumably he was denying that there would be some final end to scientific progress, some ultimate view of the world that would be literally true.

The Zhuangzi also denies this. But it does not deny that some views of the world are superior to others. The book is not relativistic any more than Kuhn is. The point of view of the cicada and the little dove is extremely limited and foolish. One of the standard objections to relativism is that, if you apply it to itself, this would seem to imply that relativism is no better than any rival view. Zhuangzi thinks that his own point of view, on the other hand, has advantages that make it worth offering to the rest of us. But the thesis that there is no ultimate definitively true view of the world does apply to the Zhuangzi. There is no suggestion that Zhuangzi's philosophy represents some final truth. The book is full of expressions of skepticism and uncertainty, along with a clear emphasis on the value of having an open mind.

Contemporary Western exponents of metaphysical anti-realism generally write in the serious style characteristic of almost all academic philosophy. Zhuangzi, though, believes that both life and one's style of communication should be changed by the insights that anti-realism affords. When people think and speak seriously, this seriousness usually appears to be guided by the ideal of capturing definitive truth, getting the world just right. If that is in fact never possible, then maybe there is something bogus about being serious?

A good deal of Daoist literature, and also that of Zen Buddhism, is infused with the idea that the indefiniteness of reality (its availability to multiple perspectives) calls for looseness and ease of response. To be serious is to fail to incorporate the anti-realist insight into one's life. It also, as we will see, is viewed as an impediment to education of the emotions.

A final point about Zhuangzi's anti-realism is this. We have seen that the anti-realist denies that, try as we might, we can arrive at a definitive and literally true description of any reality. Zhuangzi, I think, would broaden the point, applying it to nonverbal representations and to experience in general. That is, he would deny that, if a number of artists paint the same scene, any of them could possibly arrive at a "correct" or definitive representation; and he would make the same point about photographers. He also would make it about people who do not produce images of the scene at all, but merely experience it. None of us can have "the definitive" experience of any scene.

Nevertheless, there is an aestheticism at work in Zhuangzi's philosophy, which may well have contributed to a similar aestheticism later in Zen Buddhism. Zhuangzi regards the direct experience (experience, that is, apart from concepts employed and discriminations made) of reality as adding greatly to the value of life. Concepts and discriminations, though, get in the way of this direct experience, to the extent that we see things through a screen of labels and judgments. To discriminate "is to fail to see something" (Graham translation, p. 57). Anti-realism teaches us the futility of thinking that we can get reality finally right with these labels and judgments. This makes it even more pathetic, in Zhuangzi's view, that they separate us from the joy of appreciating the world.

Spontaneity

What are the advantages that Zhuangzi thinks his point of view has over those of most people? Part of the answer must be theoretical. He thinks, that is, that anti-realism (or something like it) makes better sense of the world than various realisms do.

The major advantages, though, have to do with the quality of life that is made possible if we give up on realism. Much of this quality of life can be put under the heading of emotional freedom. The major sign of this freedom will be spontaneity. We will examine Zhuangzi's view of spontaneity, and then go on to investigate how he thinks we can transform our emotional makeups in order to have better lives.

Spontaneity is sometimes thought of in terms of doing something unpredictable. Zhuangzi's view is different, centering on how something is done—especially on its spirit, and its relation to underlying states of the person who does it. The most detailed example he provides is in chapter 3. It is Cook Ding (Ting), who is fantastically good at carving meat.

A few points should be made in advance about this example. First, it is typical of Zhuangzi that the person presented as an ideal should be from a humble stratum of society, rather than some statesman or influential philosopher. However, it also should be noted that the nature of Chinese cuisine is such that carving skills matter considerably and are respected. Cook Ding is in his way very useful. He also is extremely skillful and energetic, and the suggestion is that he provides a model for skill and energy in any area of life.

When Cook Ding carves up an ox, it is as if he is doing a dance. He credits his great skill to the Way (the Dao). When he first began cutting up oxen, he would see the whole animal, but he has finally reached the point at which he moves intuitively rather than (by and large) registering consciously what his eyes see. (The Graham translation has him say that he is "in touch through the daemonic in me"). The evidence of his skill in guiding his knife through interstices is that, while a good cook changes his knife once a year, Cook Ding has had the same knife for nineteen years (and it is as good as new).

It is clear that Cook Ding is presented as an example of enlightened mysticism (the Dao) applied in daily life. Something should be said at this point about frequent Western misconceptions about Eastern mysticisms, including Daoism. Daoism certainly has a great deal to do with a peace of mind that is made possible by elimination of emotional conflicts and tensions. This might suggest the misconception that what Daoism offers is a form of relaxation therapy, freeing us from having to attend to many of the things that worry us in life. (After all, they aren't that important.)

Daoism, though, and later Zen Buddhism urge us to attend *more* to the details of life. Perhaps worry is not the best attitude in relation to them, but we do need (spiritually as well as practically) to focus more clearly on many of the little things in life. If relaxing means taking it easy by letting go of our grasp of these details, then Daoism and Zen Buddhism are against relaxation. Indeed, becoming a good Daoist or Zen Buddhist turns out to be a fairly strenuous business.

Cook Ding's carving, although it gives him joy, is hardly a matter of careless rapture. When he comes to a difficult place, he says, he pauses and examines the difficulties, keeping his eyes on what he is doing and working slowly. He carefully prepares his moves. (Note: eliminating anxiety about the future does *not* mean eliminating thought about the future, and indeed can make possible more cogent planning.)

At the end of one of these performances Cook Ding is proud and satisfied. The lord for whom he works is represented as commenting that he has learned, from Cook Ding, how to nurture life. The lessons, in other words, go beyond specific skilled activities. Life in general can be lived with skill and clarity, guided by the Dao. Or it can be the reverse.

Spontaneity certainly involves an ease of emotional expression, including the expression of emotions in skilled actions. It also connects with the notion that anyone's self has many layers, some of them going back to early childhood. Something like this idea seems to be at work in a dramatic episode in chapter 7, in which Huzi (Hu-tzu) (a Daoist teacher) has repeated encounters with a demonic shaman who is said to be exceptionally good at judging people's characters merely by looking at them. But on each occasion Huzi seems entirely different to the baffled shaman, until finally Huzi appears as himself "before we ever came out of our Ancestor . . . I attenuated, wormed in and out. Unknowing who or what we were" (Graham p. 97). At this point the shaman runs away.

It is hard to know what all of this is supposed to mean, but almost certainly part of the point is that Huzi has a multifaceted rather than a unified self (and perhaps we all do?). His final self-presentation to the shaman sounds like something from very early childhood or even from the last stage of prenatal development. Whatever it is, it is still there in Huzi's makeup. My inclination is to read into this puzzling passage the idea that these stages of self are present in all of us, but that Huzi is special in that he is very much in touch with all of the layers of his personality.

On some accounts of spontaneity, a person's relation to unconscious elements of personality is crucial. The psychiatrist Anton Ehrenzweig has linked artistic creativity to a "deceptive chaos in art's vast superstructure," and has spoken of the integration of the apparent chaos in the spontaneous freedom of creative work. Huzi apparently has some degree of control over his relation to the primitive levels of his self, and it may be that we are meant to assume that this ease of expression will carry over into all of life. Whatever he does will be spontaneous.

Too Much Goodness?

One thing that conflicts with spontaneity, in Zhuangzi's view, is a conscious emphasis on propriety. (Ehrenzweig, too, speaks of the inferiority of "academic" artists because their work is consciously guided by norms.) You can't behave in a way that is in touch with your emotions and the layers of your personality if you always are asking "Is this the right thing to do in this situation?" Systems of manners and of morality thus can rob people of naturalness and of spontaneity.

The Confucian emphasis on ritual propriety especially has this tendency. But a preoccupation with moral norms, and with being as good as you possibly can be, also undermines spontaneity. The norms become an artificial substitute for being yourself in a satisfying way.

Is Zhuangzi against virtue? There is no suggestion that he would wish people to behave in what we might think of as immoral ways. Indeed, it may well be that a trained Daoist would not violate any major moral norms: we certainly would not expect him or her to steal, rape, or murder. What Zhuangzi opposes seems to be an *attitude* toward morality—the conscious tailoring of behavior to moral norms—rather than behavior that in a natural way happens to comply with morality. Perhaps this natural compliance would count merely as ordinary, garden-variety virtue? (It certainly wouldn't be outstanding virtue.) Whatever it is, it need not conflict with spontaneity.

In chapter 2 there is a reference to the legendary time when ten suns shone (Watson p. 40; Graham p. 58). The suns are emblematic of virtue, so that ten suns are emblematic of very great virtue. The full story of the ancient myth is that there used to be ten suns, which during the old ten-day week took turns (one at a time) coming up over the earth. One day, however, all of them came up at once, beginning to burn up the world. Life on earth was saved by a superhero archer, who shot out nine of the suns.

Virtue can be excessive and dangerous. The actual human being who might have seemed to Zhuangzi to exemplify this was Confucius. Confucius appears a number of times as a character in the Zhuangzi; but it is a kind of joke-Confucius, not the real one, who is portrayed. These passages constitute a raw, not very kind parody of Confucianism.

The joke-Confucius is generally portrayed as someone half-bright, who is trying to get the hang of Daoism. He certainly does not take the keen interest in great virtue that the real Confucius did. In chapter 5, for example, the joke-Confucius praises a man who "doesn't know what his ears or eyes should approve" (Watson p. 65), to whom all things are one. The legendary Lao Tzu, later in the chapter, is portrayed as urging a character (No-Toes) to help this Confucius to see that acceptable and unacceptable are on a single string. (No-Toes, incidentally, is one of a number of characters in the book who have been mutilated as a punishment for alleged crime—and who therefore would be regarded in normal society as contemptible—but who have some genuine insight that should be respected.)

In chapter 6 there is a long passage in which the historic relation between Confucius and his favorite disciple Yen Hui is inverted. A joke-Yen Hui is portrayed as understanding something that goes beyond the joke-Confucius. Yen Hui begins by forgetting benevolence and righteousness. This repudiation of the ideal of virtue is just a start, though. Eventually Yen-Hui forgets everything, dismissing perception (by which I think is meant the self-conscious, labeling kind of perception) and intellect and casting off form.

The form to be cast off, I think, is the screen of concepts and labels that usually gets between us and the world, and that anti-realism denies has any ultimate justification. There are remarks throughout the Zhuangzi about the importance of not making distinctions. We might recall the suggestion that to discriminate is to fail to see something.

On this, as on many other topics, there is room for doubt as to how far Zhuangzi wants us to go. Does he want us entirely to eschew concepts and discriminations? This would represent a point of view more like that of the Upanishads than like anything in China. Further, Zhuangzi not only himself uses concepts; he has fun with them. This suggests that perhaps what he wants is that we soft-pedal concepts and discriminations, not giving them too much power over our thinking and experience.

In any event, eliminating or lessening the power over us of discriminations facilitates direct, unself-conscious contact with reality. This applies to moral discriminations just as much as (and perhaps even more than) to other kinds. Part of the achievement of Yen Hui's forgetting is that he has "no norms" (Graham p. 92).

Education of the Emotions

In an earlier passage, in chapter 4, Confucius is portrayed as recommending fasting of the mind/heart to Yen-Hui. This psychic fasting is of course very Daoist and goes well beyond anything that the real Confucius would have entertained. It involves a way of experiencing the world (being receptive and not relying on the customary forms and labels), and also a kind of stillness and receptiveness in relation to what one expects from the world.

A reader who has taken in Zhuangzi's emphasis on naturalness and spontaneity, as well as the Daoist scorn for moral attitudes, might wonder whether Zhuangzi's ideal world is one of primitive license. Are people supposed just to act out the various impulses that most of us keep under control? The answer is emphatically "No." The missing piece of the puzzle is fasting of the mind/heart.

To be a good Daoist is to be in harmony with the world. Anyone who has strong urges of the kind that involve craving, attachment to what is wanted, and frustration when what is wanted turns out not to be forthcoming cannot possibly maintain harmony with the world. Because of this, the Daoist attitude to desires and attachment is like Buddha's. The contexts are very different: Buddha sees the elimination of desires as key to avoidance of suffering, whereas the Daoist account puts emotional freedom and harmony with the universe in the foreground. The conceptions of self that anchor the two philosophies also are not entirely the same. But the fact remains that a good Daoist, much like a serious adherent to early Buddhist philosophy, will not be attached to anything and in that sense will not have desires.

Beneath this similarity there are some differences that are hard to formulate, including one crucial to the emotions. My sense is that the culture represented by the Daodejing and the Zhuangzi is more favorable to urges of various kinds (as long as they do not involve attachment, are not pleasure-driven, and are viewed as essentially transitory) than early Buddhist philosophy is. Be that as it may, it is clear that Zhuangzi recommends that you have an emotional life (not entire and total quietude), but also that Zhuangzi's recommended emotional life has no room for the strong emotions that involve clinging to their objects (or to the idea of their objects). These strong emotions should be eliminated in fasting of the mind/heart.

Along these lines, Confucius in chapter 4 advises someone just to go along with things and let the mind move freely. The nature of the Dao includes the fact that the world sometimes does not give us what we would have liked. An enlightened person thinks "Never mind," and goes along. That the mind move freely has a great deal to do with spontaneity and requires that one not take norms (which halt the mind in various ways) seriously.

The ability to be still is highly compatible with the mind's moving freely. Think of Cook Ding when he reaches a difficult spot. People often react too quickly to what life brings up next, especially if they are on automatic pilot. Part of being genuinely responsive to the world, though, is that sometimes one waits to respond. Nothing should force you off balance or get you to make a hurried response.

The ideal is of a calm, even life. This will have its physical side. Breathing exercises are important, and in chapter 6 it is said that the true man breathes from his heels. Presumably posture and general comportment can both reflect and reinforce the processes of enlightenment.

The calm, even life—in Zhuangzi's presentation—also has its social side. To be low-key, not anxious, and to take things as they come can contribute to personal relationships. It is significant that some enlightened or quasi-enlightened characters that appear in the Zhuangzi have spouses and families. Daoism later took new forms as a popular religion, with considerable emphasis on folk beliefs and with some of the organization characteristic of religions. At that later point, there actually were, for example, Daoist nuns. (One of the major characters in the classic Chinese opera, ca. 1600, *Peony Pavilion* was a Daoist nun.) But at the stage at which the Zhuangzi was written, there is no suggestion that a good Daoist would become something like a nun or a monk.

Instead the text suggests that Daoist skill should extend to personal relationships, even to intimate relationships. What is the secret of being really liked or loved? To be morally very virtuous is not it, nor is it simply to be good-looking. We have the case in chapter 5 of Ai T'ai-t'o, thoroughly liked by everyone who knew him, and to whom many were devoted. At least 10 women said that they would rather be Ai T'ai-t'o's concubine than another man's wife. Yet he was remarkably ugly; and he never showed the slightest sign of having an original mind, always just chiming in. But there was an extraordinary formless virtue (of a non-moral sort) to him, which communicated itself to others.

Life and Death

Not being attached to the things you want may be easier if you think that, after all, in the scheme of things they are not that important. In chapter 2 there is an amusing story that makes this point. It also has something to say about the way to deal with people who are not enlightened, who care too much.

A keeper of monkeys gives each monkey three rations of nuts in the morning and four at night. The monkeys become very angry, at which the keeper offers to give them four in the morning and three at night. This makes the monkeys happy.

This is a parable for the things we care about. The monkeys' reactions to the two alternative schedules of nut delivery are out of proportion to the difference between them. Similarly, perhaps we care about things that—seen in reasonable perspective—do not make all that much difference?

The story of the monkeys and the keeper is more complicated than it first looks, because the responses of the keeper also are meant to suggest something important about life. The keeper stands in for a sage who (Watson p. 36) "harmonizes . . . walking two roads." The two roads presumably are (1) the path of personal enlightenment, and (2) that of entering into the mind-set of others (who are definitely not enlightened). The imperfection in people's understanding of the Way is how love becomes complete. Much as the monkey keeper accommodates the monkeys, so a good Daoist will accommodate those around her or him. This touches on a subject already discussed: Daoism in personal relationships.

The parable of the monkeys may look as plausible as it does because so clearly what the monkeys get in the end is, whatever the schedule of nut delivery, the same. Perhaps there are larger concerns that are not so easy to represent as not really important? The most obvious candidate is death. Even if we can say "Three in the morning and four at night, or four in the morning and three at night: big deal!" it is not so easy to say "My death: big deal!"

The topic of death comes up again and again in the Zhuangzi. As in the case of the monkey keeper and the monkeys, there is a double message. On one hand, a good Daoist is expected to have a low-key preference for remaining alive. Daoism teaches poise, and emotional freedom that carries with it the elimination of inner conflict This is held to be conducive to long life. The connection between Daoism and survival became highlighted as Daoism evolved from a countercultural philosophy to a status as a popular religion, which often talked about immortality. But there are suggestions even in the Zhuangzi of a connection between Daoism and peaceful long life. In chapter 6, for example, it is said that someone who has heard the Way can be old in years and yet have the complexion of a child.

Above and beyond this, there are strategies that may prolong life. Zhuangzi has no hesitation in recommending these. One strategy is that of being useless. In chapter 1 and in chapter 4 there is the metaphor of the tree that escapes being cut down because its wood is useless. In chapter 4 there also is the story of the lucky cripple who escapes being dragged off to war or to compulsory work projects. The reader is meant to think that those who are too useful to the state, becoming high officials, are likely to have shortened lives and should have learned the lesson of uselessness.

So long life definitely is recommended. On the other hand, the very peace of mind that is conducive to long life requires that one not seriously care about death. This does not preclude careful self-protection, such as avoiding tigers in the wild or high political office (the glittering honor that the Zhuangzi regards as being as hazardous to life and health as tigers are). Remember how Cook Ding could plan his moves, when he reached a difficult point in cutting meat, without being anxious about or attached to the results. In much this way, you can plan strategies of survival and good health without being anxious about, or attached to, life and good health. You can *take care*—in the sense of looking ahead, and focusing clearly on risks and complications—without *deeply caring* (in the sense that involves tension and attachment).

You are not supposed deeply to care about death, and this attitude can be expected to be contagious. In chapter 2 it is said that the perfect man does not care about life and death. At the end of chapter 3 it is suggested that if the people around you are deeply upset over your death, that in a way reveals a limitation of your nature. (You should have communicated calmer attitudes to them.) Everyone dies, and there should be no room for grief and joy to enter in. In the rhythms of the world, Lao Tzu is made to say in chapter 5, life and death are the same story.

Chapter 6 contains the most ample and rhapsodic discussion of death (Graham pp. 87–89; Watson pp. 80–82). Four friends are described as agreeing on the mutual interrelationship of life and death. Then one of them becomes ill in a way that grotesquely transforms his body. But he remains calm, speculating cheerfully on the strange things that may happen to his body. A second becomes terminally ill. His visiting friend brushes aside a weeping wife and children and chats with the dying man about the transformation that is about to occur. It is hard to know what form this will take. Perhaps the dying man (i.e., part of him) will become a rat's liver, or the limb of an insect?

The entire passage is filled with surreal and colorful imagery. But it may well leave some readers puzzled, in part because a great deal of philosophy is at work—but the philosophy is beneath the surface, rather than explicit. Certainly the passage is predicated on the rejection of what often nowadays is referred to as Cartesian dualism, the view that mind and body are two entirely separate entities. Zhuangzi appears to equate the dying men with their bodies.

There also may seem to be a religious or quasi-religious underpinning to this discussion of death. Zhuangzi refers to a creator or maker of the world. My sense is that the reference should be taken at face value, but that it also is a speculation on Zhuangzi's part: hardly anything is said elsewhere about this creator or maker. Part of Zhuangzi's anti-realism, it should be recalled, is the insistence that there are no final truths, not even in what he says. This leads to the point that there is a great deal that we simply do not know and perhaps are not in a position to know. Perhaps, he says in chapter 2, there will be a great awakening at which we will know that our present experience was all a dream. This sense of the limitations of human knowledge does not preclude having beliefs and opinions, and the reference in chapter 6 may indicate one of these.

The rhapsody on death also involves the word "transform," as in the thought that after death my right arm may be transformed into who-knows-what. The thought may look casual. But it is connected to one of most distinctive elements in Daoist philosophy, which in turn has a crucial role in attitudes toward death and also in the general account of reality.

This is the idea of the transformation of things. It had appeared earlier in the work, at the end of chapter 3. There occurs the most famous passage in the Zhuangzi. In it Zhuangzi has dreamt that he is a butterfly, and on "awakening" wonders whether he is in fact a butterfly now dreaming he is a human being, or a human being who has just dreamt that he is a butterfly.

A Western reader may be reminded of the concern in the *Meditations* of the seventeenth-century philosopher Rene Descartes over whether you can know that you are not dreaming. Perhaps you can't know? Descartes thinks that this would destroy the possibility of having any knowledge, apart from the knowledge that you yourself exist. To his relief, though, he is able to come up with a chain of proofs (themselves highly controversial) that would appear to show that we can know.

Chapter 2 makes it clear that Zhuangzi would take the side of "can't know." But there is more to the discussion of the dream than this. In a teasing way Zhuangzi remarks that, of course, there must be a difference between being a butterfly and being a human being. The tone is significant: teasing and irony are the tropes of someone who has adjusted her or his speech to anti-realism. The final sentence of the chapter is especially significant. This (the difference between being a butterfly and being a human being), Zhuangzi says, is called the transformation(s) of things.

The Transformation of Things

The simplest explanation is that human beings, after they die, sometimes become parts of butterflies, and vice versa. If we take a snapshot view of the world, then humans and butterflies are quite distinct. If, however, we assume that the nature of anything cannot be supplied by a snapshot, and that instead we need a longitudinal view (through time), then the distinction between humans and butterflies can look less sharp.

At the heart of Daoist metaphysics is the embrace of time. Time of course is connected with change, decay, and death. This is enough to give many of us an ambivalent attitude toward time. It would be nice if certain things stayed the same, and perhaps even better if one could go backward. A major Western philosophy, that of Plato, has erected a great structure over this ambivalence, exalting being (the object of any true knowledge, in Plato's view) and de-emphasizing becoming.

Daoism, in contrast, offers a metaphysics of becoming. The world offers a rich and exciting swirl of qualities and states, constantly changing. No other major philosophy conveys so well the pleasure of the new, and the importance of openness to it. Nature is ever new, always various.

There is a wonderful evocation of this at the beginning of chapter 2, beginning with the "pipes of Heaven" (Graham p. 48). This long passage is a riff on the movements and noises of inanimate nature. You have to love it, the text seems to say. But the suggestion also is that this vitality and vibrancy, rather than some still timelessness, is the true nature of reality.

Confucius (for once being made to sound like a fully enlightened Daoist) speaks in chapter 5 of how life and death, and all of the other things that matter a lot to most people, should be seen simply as alterations of the world. This follows immediately on the story of Ai

T'ai-t'o, the exceptionally ugly man to whom many are devoted. Presumably Ai T'ai-t'o in some way understands how all of these ups and downs are merely transformations of the world, and perhaps his having come to terms with this is the secret of his appeal. As Confucius remarks, there is no reason that all the changes in the world should be "enough to destroy your harmony" (Watson p. 70).

Instead, the passage insists, the transformation of things should be a source of joy. Indeed, you should mingle with it, merging with the moment in your own mind. This is at the heart of the Zhuangzi's vision of what it is to be in harmony with the Dao.

Conclusion

The Zhuangzi is a philosophical counterpart to fireworks. Brightly colored lines of thought go off in many directions. Nevertheless, there is a structure, which includes implicit argument.

Here are a few lines of argument.

1. Whatever truth about something we think we have reached, alternative perspectives (yielding different results) are available.
2. We cannot rule out the possibility that one of these perspectives is superior to ours.
3. Even if we have good reason to reject the suggestion that any currently available alternative perspective is superior to ours, we cannot rule out the possibility that a superior one will become available.
4. Therefore we can never be in a position to claim a final, optimal version of truth about anything.

Also,

5. Seriousness is justified only if there is a final, optimal truth to be found or to be promoted.
6. But there is never any realistic prospect of finding or promoting a final, optimal truth.
7. Therefore seriousness is never justified.

Also,

8. What we can see of people's lives suggests that certain kinds of emotions—the ones that attach themselves to people and objects, in such a way that not getting what one wants will lead to frustration or suffering—create unsatisfactory lives.

9. The seriousness that No. 7 concluded was never justified also leads to a kind of rigidity of thought that makes it difficult to feel harmonious with new and hard-to-categorize developments in the world.

10. Someone who, conversely, can harmonize with changes in the world without conceptual strain, and without attachments or risks of suffering, can find the rhythms of the world very gratifying.

11. Therefore fasting of the mind-heart, which loosens the grip on us of familiar conceptual structures and also dwindles emotions of attachment, makes possible a gratifying harmony with the world.

The foregoing should be seen as a crude approximation to some major elements in the text. Clearly the Zhuangzi is not, in any overt way, an argumentative work. Zhuangzi would like the reader or hearer to arrive at a more liberated and satisfying style of life. You don't argue people into something like that. Arguments, in fact, like morality, would be from the Daoist point of view highly likely to be counterproductive. If someone is to see the good sense in Daoism, and the genuine appeal of a Daoist style of life, then that person must come to it of herself or himself, rather than be pushed into it by arguments. The Zhuangzi, instead of overtly arguing for its views, is full of hints, suggestions, and joky or surprising forms of writing that are designed to shake up the reader's thinking and to make change more possible.

Nevertheless, Zhuangzi has his reasons for everything that he suggests or seems to believe. In that sense he has arguments. Arriving at a philosophical understanding of what goes on in the text requires grasping what these arguments are. This makes philosophical understanding a somewhat different process from that of opening one's mind to whatever the appeal of Zhuangzi's thought might be. But one activity does not preclude the other, and indeed the process of philosophical understanding—if it is undertaken in the right spirit—always can be conducive to an opening of the mind to new ways of thinking.

Recommended Reading

There are at least two very good translations of the Zhuangzi. See *Chuang Tzu, Basic Writings,* trans. Burton Watson (New York: Columbia University Press, 1964), and *The Seven Inner Chapters and Other Writings from the Book Chuang Tzu,* trans. A. C. Graham (London: Geo. Allen & Unwin, 1981). I slightly prefer the Graham translation. There also is a comic book version: *Zhuangzi Speaks,* trans. Brian Bruya (Princeton: Princeton University Press, 1992).

Two essays that do an excellent job of clarifying obscurities and disputed points in the Zhuangzi are Philip J. Ivanhoe, "Skepticism, Skill and the Ineffable Tao," *Journal of the American Academy of Religions* 61 (1993), 639–54; and Bryan Van Norden, "Competing Interpretations of the Inner Chapters of the Zhuangzi," *Philosophy East and West* 46 (1996), 247–68.

T. S. Kuhn's "Reply to My Critics" is contained in *Criticism and the Growth of Knowledge,* ed. Imre Lakatos and Alan Musgrave (Cambridge: Cambridge University Press, 1970).

Anton Ehrenzweig's *The Hidden Order of Art* (Berkeley: University of California Press, 1967) offers an interesting look at creativity in the arts; but it also harmonizes very well with much that is in the Zhuangzi.

EIGHT

ZEN FLESH, ZEN BONES

Zen Flesh, Zen Bones is a collection of anecdotes and incidents connected with Zen Buddhism, many of them several hundred years old and originating in China. Most in fact represent Chinese Chan Buddhism, which in Japan became known as Zen. They are pungent, frequently amusing, and to all appearances not at all systematic. In this chapter we will explore them along with a classic Chan text, the Platform Sutra, that is in a way systematic.

Here is a story from *Zen Flesh, Zen Bones*. It is No. 1 in The Gateless Gate, the second part of the book. A monk asks a Chinese Chan/Zen master whether a dog has Buddha nature or not. The master replies "mu," which means something like "nothingness." Six paragraphs of comment follow, which basically say that this is an extremely important problem. Great energy and persistence are required to penetrate the meaning of "mu," but if you can do it this will transform your life.

The first-time reader may well have a sense of mystification. Something is going on, but what is it? Many of the stories in *Zen Flesh, Zen Bones* have a bit more surface meaning than the one just cited. There is, for example, the parable of the man pursued by a tiger over a cliff, finally hanging on to a dangling vine, which then is being chewed at by two mice. What does the man do? He eats a strawberry. Clearly there is something deeper here than the surface meaning. But what is it?

Is There Philosophy Here?

Does Zen amount to a philosophy? This is almost as difficult a question as whether it amounts to a religion. In both cases it pushes at the borderline of a category. As a religion Zen looks very odd indeed. There is no theology, no creed. Most scholars would say that this is true also of Buddha's original teaching (thus placing in doubt whether Buddha's Buddhism counts as a religion), but certainly some forms of later Buddhism have been prepared to make serious claims about the afterlife that were far less guarded than Buddha's remarks on the subject. This element is absent from Zen, in which there is nothing—about gods, semidivine beings, or an afterlife—to believe.

On the other hand, Zen does contain a pervasive, integrated vision of how it is best to live, which is an important element of what we regard as the great world religions. The vision is linked to teaching designed to give access to deeper truths than the average person is aware of: this again is characteristic of some major religions. Further, Zen has styles of organization, including monasteries, like those of religions. In China, where Zen originated as Chan Buddhism, there even were patriarchs, heads of the Zen movement. The Platform Sutra is the work of the sixth patriarch.

Is Zen a philosophy? The reader should bear in mind both the central role of argument in what we would consider to be philosophy, and also that the argument (as in some of the philosophies discussed earlier in this book) can be largely implicit rather than explicit. There is very little explicit argument in Zen texts. The Platform Sutra does have, as I will try to show, a structure of implicit argument. The texts, mostly pretty short, that are included in *Zen Flesh, Zen Bones* are a more complicated matter. In some of the philosophies analyzed in previous chapters it is as if there are arguments between the lines. In the Zen stories it is as if the arguments had been given earlier, and then had been digested and gone beyond. There is a strong philosophical element in these stories, and I will try to bring it out. But the stories dramatize (rather than explain) the philosophical element. It is as if the Zen teachers are saying, "This is how a philosophy can enter people's lives, and now we are getting on with life."

By and large the philosophical moves that give rise to Zen Buddhism indeed had been made earlier, although their use in Zen added some twists and nuances. Clearly the classic texts of Daoism, especially the Zhuangzi, contributed a great deal to Chan (and then Zen) Buddhism. For that matter, Buddha's original teaching does play a major role. Finally, there is a significant contribution from an earlier school of Buddhist philosophy, Madhyamika, the major figure in which was Nagarjuna.

Nagarjuna's writings are full of explicit philosophical arguments. The method is resolutely negative. Nagarjuna denies the absoluteness of all philosophical standpoints, again and again undercutting conceptual distinctions, without endorsing the standpoint of his own in any clear-cut way. To the extent that there is a philosophical idea that survives this argumentative blitz, it is the idea of *Shunyata* (*Sunyata*), usually translated as emptiness—although it may be that it has connections with our idea of openness, and also with indeterminacy.

A Zen idea that seems very like *shunyata* is one we have already encountered, *"mu."* At first blush *mu* seems a negative, but a peculiarly noncommital negative. In his admirably clear book on Zen, Thomas Kasulis glosses *mu* (p. 13) as "a refusal to accept the conceptual distinctions which give the question meaning." It can be viewed as a demand to think behind the words of the question, rather to take the question at face value. In the philosophical tradition that stems from Madhyamika, all linguistic distinctions are regarded as ultimately unacceptable. But usually there is no harm in using them in talking, as long as they are (as it were) held out at arm's length. Occasionally, though, the unacceptability of conceptual distinctions needs to be emphasized. It is on those occasions that *"mu"* is appropriate.

Let us go back to the question of the dog's Buddha nature. "Buddha nature" has something to do with raw spiritual potential. D. T. Suzuki, the great scholar of Zen, equates it roughly with self-nature (the underlying nature of self) and with *shunyata*. In some ways it would be misleading to say that a dog has Buddha nature. Dogs are not quite persons. But, insofar as spiritual potential has something to do with personality, anyone who knows dogs knows that it also would be misleading simply to deny that a dog has Buddha nature. This is one of those moments at which an intelligent person should avoid imposing ready-made categories (whether positive or negative) on reality. The labels get in the way of direct experience.

Anti-Realism

The contemporary philosophical position that has the closest resemblance with that explicitly argued for by Nagarjuna, and implicit in the Zen literature, is metaphysical anti-realism. It was discussed in the last chapter because the philosophy of the Zhuangzi also is, in current terms, strongly anti-realist. Anti-realism functions in Zen, as we will see, as the starting point for some positive guidance in life.

Contemporary anti-realists occasionally have given their position a dramatic turn, by denying that there is a world or a reality to be experienced. What is denied, however (by philosophers like Richard Rorty), is the notion of a world with an objective nature, which then would be mirrored by entirely true accounts of it. It is hard to deny that we experience *something,* even if it turns out that there is no final and definitive account of the nature of that something.

Call the something we experience the world. The core of metaphysical anti-realism is the insistence that different accounts or views of the world always are possible. Some accounts of it may be more perspicacious and reliable than others. The anti-realist philosopher of science Thomas Kuhn, for example, insisted that there is scientific progress and that the world cannot be fit into an arbitrary set of conceptual boxes. But scientific progress is regarded as compatible with the claim that there is no ideal, final science that perfectly mirrors the reality it describes.

The great figures of Asian anti-realism are Zhuangzi and Nagarjuna, and the latter does provide elaborate structures of explicit argument. Zhuangzi more closely anticipates Zen Buddhism in one respect. He links infatuation with conceptual labels (for what is experienced) with impoverishment of experience. To insist on finding the right labels, he remarks, is to fail to see something. The unique sensuous qualities, that is, fade from experience as labels are noted.

Much of the problem reflects a struggle between convenience, on one hand, and richness of experience, on the other, that convenience generally wins. When I walk in the autumn from my office to a classroom, I generally do not take in the shapes and tints of leaves on the trees that I pass, or the formation of clouds in the sky. One is aware that there are trees. There certainly is the basic awareness involved in not bumping into one of them, and incipient rain also will be noted. It is as if the world calls out, as you walk by, "Tree there to the left; tree on the right; about to rain . . ." This kind of thing allows us to get through life quickly and efficiently.

What is lost is the beauty of what we are going by. To savor and appreciate this beauty requires—for us, who are sickled over with concepts—a positive effort of attention. It takes time and mental energy. In this respect it is highly inefficient; and it is no wonder that the immediate (and rather unstructured) sensous experience of a small child is gradually replaced, as the child gets older, by a repertoire of labels.

One might think that this is not such a great loss. Perhaps the leaves on the trees on a New England campus in autumn have real aesthetic appeal. But much of life is spent in rooms with peeling paint, or on dingy and cluttered city streets. Perhaps seeing all of this through labels, rather than with sensuous detail, is merciful as well as efficient?

The Zen reply to this appeals to a little-appreciated facet of anti-realism, and also to an optimism about human capabilities. Metaphysical anti-realism tells us that a multitude of perspectives on, or accounts of, any reality will be possible; there is no objective mirroring that gives a definitive version. This opens the door to the thought that anything, seen well, can be beautiful. This idea is familiar to artists, who have sometimes arrived at beautiful representations of what most people would think of as rather ugly. A good example is the Rembrandt painting in the Louvre in Paris of a side of beef. The thought then, in short, is that if you really look at something, in an unhurried way taking in sensuous detail, you can see it as beautiful. It may take practice, but it is possible.

The awareness of detail is crucial to this process. That is, someone who really looks (in a good way) at the world can be expected not to experience a vague gestalt of beauty, but rather to see a complex and intriguing interconnectedness of clearly noted particulars. The importance of detail emerges in one story (no. 35 of 101 Zen Stories, the first part of Zen Flesh). A Zen teacher goes to visit his old master on a rainy day, leaving his shoes and umbrella in the vestibule. The old master then asks him whether his umbrella is on the right or the left side of the shoes. With a shock, the teacher realizes that he does not know and goes back to being a pupil for another six years.

Plainly the clarity of experience that Zen promises is not easily won. Nevertheless, there is the optimistic assumption that anyone who can make significant progress in Zen training will find more clarity and beauty in her or his experience. Worries, preoccupations, and, above all, those seemingly useful but pesky conceptual labels get in the way of our appreciating the beauty that is available to us. Zen training eliminates the major impediments and opens us up to the world.

This is a program of learning to live in a world of particularity—a world never quite captured by words—that gives an added dimension to the suggestion in the Daodejing that the Way is gained by daily loss. The daily loss is naturally thought of as loss of worries and preoccupations, and assorted emotional baggage connected with these.

But—certainly in the Zen version—there also must be a loss of the habit of experiencing the world through a screen of conceptual labels. The whole tendency of education from early childhood on needs to be reversed. We need to loosen the hold on us of conceptualized awareness of the world.

Conceptualized awareness will not be totally eliminated. Rather it will be treated with irony and humor, and subordinated to direct experience of sensuous particularity. But on occasion it is perfectly all right to use the labels that we learned in growing up.

There is a Zen story (no. 89 of 101 Stories) that nicely illustrates this, along with the way in which so much of Zen dialogue is thought of as improvisatory riffs rather than as attempts at replicating some putatively objective structure of reality. Two Zen temples each had a child protégé, who would meet and exchange words on their way to get vegetables in the morning. On one occasion, when the first child asked the second, "Where are you going?" the reply was "I am going wherever my feet go." The first child went to his teacher for coaching, who said that next time when the second child said that, he should say, "Suppose you have no feet, then where are you going?" But the next day the second child, asked where he was going, replied, "I am going wherever the wind blows." The day after this, the first child again asked where the second was going, this time prepared with a question about what if there is no wind. But this time the unanswerable reply was "I am going to market to buy vegetables."

A great deal of Zen training has to be understood as designed to facilitate this freedom with (and from) concepts. Sitting in meditation takes one away from the brisk, practical mind-set that leads to excessive reliance on established labels. At the same time meditation can promote an openness of the mind. Then there are the Zen puzzles (koans), such as the famous question "What is the sound of one hand clapping?" These call for a fluidity of thought, more like improvisation than like playing a scale. There is no remotely plausible literal answer to the question about one hand clapping, and thus this koan gets across the way in which a view of the world need not attempt to be some literal rendering of a definitive reality.

Humor has a major role in the educational process. Humor is, first of all, sometimes more effective than simple rejection in undermining entrenched attitudes (including those linked to the false idea of literal truth). But also the experience of someone who has learned to reject the false ideals of realism can involve rapid shifts of perspective, which will have the incongruity characteristic of much humor. Zen also promotes the sense that all of life, including all speech and experience, is a kind of improvisation. This implies that you do not take yourself at all seriously and leads to a kind of lightheartedness.

On some occasions Zen parodies itself. There is a comic version (no. 26 of 101 Zen Stories) of a debate in mime between a wandering monk (seeking lodging at a temple) and a monk who lived there. The latter (the resident monk) was stupid and had only one eye. The wandering monk first held up one finger, representing Buddha; the resident monk held up two fingers, which the visitor took to represent Buddha and his teaching. The wandering monk then held up three fingers, to represent Buddha, his teaching, and the harmonious community; the resident monk then shook his clenched fish in the visitor's face, seeming to indicate the origin of the three elements from one realization. The visiting monk conceded defeat. But—it turned out— the resident monk had interpreted the one finger as "You have only one eye." His two fingers were a polite way of congratulating the visitor on having two eyes, but then he took the three fingers to say "Yes, between us we have three eyes." His rage had no bounds: hence the clenched fist.

Plainly the process of taking reality as indeterminate, subject to multiple perspectives, can get out of hand. It also can lead to a pompous, excessively complicated way of thinking. There is a story of a monk who traveled to the south in order to teach others what he had learned (no. 28 in The Gateless Gate). On the way he stopped and asked an old woman for tea and refreshments. She asked what his heavy burden was; and he replied that it was a commentary that he had written over many years, on a sutra (a Buddhist sacred text). To this she remarked, "I have read that sutra which says 'The past mind cannot be held, the present mind cannot be held, the future mind cannot be held.' You wish some tea and refreshments. Which mind do you propose to use for them?" The monk was stunned. Having suddenly gained humility, he realized that he needed much more teaching.

Zen certainly eschews pompous formulations. Instead there is a decided preference for the brief, apt comment. Anti-realists will have to believe that any comment on anything cannot claim to be the definitive, literal truth. There always is room for other perspectives, and hence any comment must be in a sense one-sided. Long pompous formulations, though, usually come across with the air of pretending to be definitive. The very brief, snappy comment—precisely because it is brief—has the air, on the other hand, of being the first word, and of not being intended to include the last word.

Story 29 in The Gateless Gate dramatizes nicely the use of the brief and apt comment. Two monks argue about a flag. One says, "The flag is moving." The other says, "The wind is moving." The sixth patriarch happens to walk by and remarks, "Not the wind, not the flag; mind is moving."

No one would take this to be literal truth. All three parties are right, in a way. It depends on the point of view, and in that sense mind is moving.

The brief comment, in short, can be taken as gesturing at something that never will be adequately captured in words. It is something like a first step in a journey, to be followed by more words or (even better) by increased clarity of experience and reflection. First steps that are quite different from one another can each be useful, depending on the context and what is to follow. This is illustrated by no. 30 and no. 33 in The Gateless Gate, in which a Zen teacher on one occasion says, "This mind is Buddha," and on another occasion says, "This mind is not Buddha."

Zen Buddhists are certainly not against words. The Zen texts are full of words, much of this displaying verbal agility. But if we abandon the idea that words definitively can mirror an objective reality, then we are left with the thought that at best words gesture at what we can experience—and at movements of the mind in relation to this experience. Gestures without words also can do this, expressing orientations toward the world. A Zen version of a sermon that Buddha might have delivered (no. 6 in The Gateless Gate) has Buddha simply turning a flower in his fingers, and saying nothing. Presumably bodily posture and facial expression were an important part of the message. In this version, only one person watching him understood the "revelation." The comment that follows this sermon is (characteristically for Zen) ironic and irreverent. Communication, of any kind, doesn't always work.

A Matter-of-Fact Attitude toward the World

The characteristic Zen attitude toward life is best appreciated in relation to death. Let us return to the story of the man who is pursued over a cliff by a hungry tiger, and who is left hanging from a vine that turns out to have two mice chewing it. One mouse is black and the other is white. In the Zen world of fluidity of meanings, there generally is room for varying interpretations of anything. But in this case it is likely that the two mice are intended to symbolize night and day, and that the point is that the unending rhythm of night and day inevitably eats away at anyone's life. The man hanging from the vine will die, as will we all. Zen, you should recall, has nothing to say about any life after death. If the man hanging from the vine reaches for a strawberry and eats it, that suggests an ethics of making the most of the moments one has. I will discuss the ramifications of this ethics shortly.

Meanwhile there is the topic of death. The great French aphorist the Duc de La Rochefoucauld compared thinking about death to staring at the sun. Both, he thought, are well-nigh impossible to continue for any length of time. But it remains the case that what you make of death will determine much in your attitude toward life. Most of us deeply fear death. The Zen attitude appears to be instead that no special emotion toward death makes sense. It is simply a fact of life.

No. 78 in 101 Zen Stories brings this out nicely. A rich man asks a Zen monk to write out something that calls for the well-being of his family. The monk writes "Father dies; son dies; grandson dies." When the rich man expostulates, the monk points out that he could hardly prefer any other order. If the son dies before the father, or the grandson before the son, hearts will be broken.

What does this leave us with? No. 19 of The Gateless Gate gives a short answer. Everyday life is the path. This makes two points simultaneously. One is that, given the facts of life and death, we should simply live—and make the most of even the odd, seemingly uneventful parts of life. The second point (which we will now explore) is that what Zen can offer is not some magical transformation that dramatically alters life so that it assumes an undreamt-of intensity. The payoff will be a life that, as various Zen texts promise, can be deeply satisfying. But to the casual observer it will seem like an ordinary life.

Every-Minute Value

At this point, some readers will wonder whether the Zen ethic is one of casual hedonism. They may be reminded of an old commercial for beer which began, "If you go around only once . . ." Eating the strawberry while dangling from the vine might be taken to be like partying on the edge of disaster.

This is very far from the ethics of Zen, although there is no doubt that Zen Buddhists believe that there is—or can be—a sweetness in life, as symbolized by the strawberry. The echoes in the Zen texts of past philosophy include not only metaphysical anti-realism but also the arguments, in early Buddhist texts such as the Dhammapada, against desire and any search for pleasure. These arguments would be very familiar in any Buddhist country. There was no need to repeat them.

Having desires and looking for pleasure would be regarded as somewhat like savoring a toxic strawberry. Pleasures inevitably create attachments and vulnerability to suffering. Desires entail periods of frustration before a desire is satisfied, and also boredom as the satisfaction wears off and new desires have not yet fully formed. The Buddhist solution (outlined in chapter 2) is to have mild preferences that lack the attachment and intensity characteristic of desire, and to have satisfactions that are not keyed to objects or to craving. These satisfactions will be more like joy than pleasure. There is nothing in any Zen text to suggest that this traditional Buddhist pattern of thought is not accepted.

We can savor what we experience without being attached to specific objects and experiences. This can amount to a joyful attitude of "We will take what comes." Whatever comes can be experienced positively. No. 31 of 101 Zen Stories relates the awakening of a Zen monk who overheard a conversation between a butcher and a customer who asked for the best piece of the meat. The butcher replied that everything in his shop was the best. This attitude can be extended to all of life, which can be joyful even if there are no special high points or moments of special excitement. The early Buddhist logic that insists that high points imply low points is very much in the background of this line of thought.

The story that immediately follows the tale of the butcher concerns a lord much of whose life is spent in sitting stiffly to receive the ritual homage of others. All of this is dreary. The lord asks a Zen teacher for help and is given a poem. The gist of the poem is that no moment will be repeated, and that each moment should be precious.

As advice this may seem short on specifics. But clearly the thought is that the lord's life can be brightened and made more satisfying, not by some dramatic breakthrough, but rather by a deepening of each immediate experience. One can make an effort of attention to be more sensitive to the beauty of the textures of the moment. Presumably also, the lord's posture and words can be adjusted by subtle nuances of style, so that he is no longer sitting and behaving stiffly. There is a lot that can be done even with such unpromising materials as ritual interactions.

If the Zen teacher's poem is short on specifics, this is in part because it is very hard to formulate stylistic subtleties. There is no readily available vocabulary that will do them justice. But it is also that whatever the lord does to make his moments of sitting meaningful and satisfying will have to be something he comes to of himself. There is no codebook in which one can look up how to have a meaningful life. The Zen teacher merely can point out the possibility and gesture at the directions that might be taken.

Toward the end of *Zen Flesh, Zen Bones* there is a Zen illustrated story, "The Search for the Bull," adapted from an earlier Daoist version. The bull that is sought for represents something like an authentic self. In the final panel, the Zen central character is portrayed both as blissful and as, in effect, disappearing into the crowd. Part of the comment is "The beauty of my garden is invisible." Whatever Zen has to offer will not be easily recognized by the average person as something wonderful and enviable, and it may not be noticed that someone has it. But unnoticed bliss is bliss nonetheless.

Emotional Change

On the way to bliss, you need to become a different kind of person. Zen texts emphasize differences in performance and in insight, especially in responses to the ever-changing circumstances of life. Clearly, though, there also are characteristic changes in someone's emotional makeup.

A natural thought is that emotional changes will include, as a major element, the elimination of unworthy emotions, such as anger, lust, and, more generally, desires. There has been, in the traditions that are most familiar in the West, a strong connection between spiritual progress and purification. But we should remember that Buddha's teaching also was focused on a kind of purification, namely the elimination of desire (which includes eliminating unselfish desires as well as selfish ones).

In the light of this, it might be tempting to think of a spiritual life, as a rival of the sixth patriarch did, as rather like keeping dust off a mirror (the mirror of the mind). Many Zen texts, though, point toward a much more qualified and complicated account. Indeed, it is sometimes suggested that, while an emphasis on purification can have some beneficial results, it essentially is a low-level and limited program of development.

Certainly, rejecting aspects of oneself can be enormously risky. It sets off conflicts and disturbances. No. 14 of 101 Zen Stories illustrates this. Two monks traveling along a muddy road in heavy rain encounter a lovely young woman in a silk kimono who is unable to cross an intersection. One monk simply picks up the woman in his arms and carries her over the mud, then sets her down. (This, it should be noted, is on the face of it a rather unmonklike thing to do.) The second monk fumes silently for hours, and then finally reminds the first that monks are supposed to avoid women (especially young and lovely ones). The reply is "I left the girl there. Are you still carrying her?"

This certainly does not mean that the serious Zen monk or nun will cheerfully maintain a level of lustful thoughts that would be characteristic of many laypersons. My sense is that such thoughts could be expected naturally to dwindle and fade amidst the routines of Zen training. But this withering away is quite different from what would be involved if the monk or nun carried on a struggle with lustful thoughts, a struggle that would be bound to be counterproductive.

This possibly is related to part of the meaning of a fable that is No. 2 of The Gateless Gate. A Zen teacher encounters a fox, who reveals that in a past life he was a Zen master who had been asked whether or not the enlightened man is subject to the law of causation. He had replied in the negative, and for this "clinging to absoluteness" he had been condemned to five hundred lifetimes as a fox. He can be saved from living in a fox's body if the Zen teacher gives him a good answer to the question of whether the enlightened man is subject to the law of causation.

The successful answer (which the Western philosopher Baruch Spinoza would have liked) was neither positive nor negative, but rather that the enlightened man is one with the law of causation. The point is that, even if we all are governed by laws of cause and effect, there is a big difference between, on one hand, someone who is governed by these as something coming from outside her or his personality, and, on the other hand, someone who (through the causation of a superior psychological adjustment) harmonizes urges and behavior with these laws. The enlightened person is at ease in the universe.

This can be true in relation to the most primal elements of life. No. 80 of 101 Zen Stories reports an incident in which a Zen teacher is challenged by someone from another Buddhist sect, whose founder was alleged to have performed miracles. My miracle, the Zen teacher retorts, is that when I feel hungry I eat, and when I feel thirsty I drink.

Stories of this sort cannot be taken too simply. There is no suggestion that, if the only food immediately available is on someone else's plate, the Zen teacher would grab it. Nor would someone who had undergone Zen training be likely to experience hunger and thirst the way that, say, the average two-year-old would.

What is suggested, I think, is twofold. First, it is assumed as obvious that various urges and appetites will be modified or will lessen in force as a result of the spiritual discipline of Zen training. But clearly some will remain, including most obviously hunger or thirst. How the Zen initiate will respond to these will depend on circumstances. Zen teaches a high degree of sensitivity and responsiveness to the world, which includes of course the social situations one finds oneself in. In no case, however, will a response be simply a matter of struggling with one's urges, and in normal circumstances urges (such as hunger and thirst) will be expressed with a natural ease that dramatically goes beyond what is available to most of us.

Enlightenment

Much of what we have been discussing as the goals of Zen teaching looks like a matter of degree. It might seem that bliss could be experienced more often or less often, and that the poise and fluidity prized by Zen Buddhists could be displayed in finer forms by some adepts than by others. That this is the case is suggested also by the way in which, when the position of head of a monastery is open, a few monks will be much stronger candidates than others.

Nevertheless, there is something aimed for (*satori*, generally translated as enlightenment) that is presented as not a matter of degree. Initially the student of Zen does not have it, and then (if everything goes well) he or she does have it. One of the divisions between the two major schools of Zen, Soto and Rinzai, is that the former treats the attainment of enlightenment as a gradual process and the latter presents it as sudden and dramatic. A Rinzai example is the case, described earlier, of the Zen monk who was suddenly awakened when he heard a butcher claim that everything in his shop was the best (a message that could be extended to everything in life).

The accounts of enlightenment most widely read in the West are those of the Rinzai (sudden enlightenment) school. These make it sound as if enlightenment was like a sudden clearing away of psychic blockage. (The word "psychic" has to be taken here in a broad sense, in which it includes features of behavior and even posture; we will explore this shortly.) The Zen student has been, as it were, tangled up with himself or herself, unable to act in a fluid and conflict-free way. Suddenly there is a sense of freedom, of obstacles removed, and of harmony with oneself. The immediate experience of this transformation (as portrayed in the Rinzai texts) is dramatic, and clearly feels great.

Some readers might think of Zen enlightenment as a matter of the mind (or the soul) entering a higher state. This view of it is congenial within a Western tradition, which goes back to Plato and includes the "dualism" of Descartes, that sharply separates the soul or mind from the body. In this traditional view, we are a compound of two different kinds of substance. The purification of the soul may well have effects on the body; but these effects will be indirect, bridging the gap between two different kinds of substance.

This dualist view remains arguable, although very many Western philosophers nowadays are inclined to reject it. In any event, there is no suggestion that Zen Buddhists viewed the mind and the body entirely as separate realities. The words "mind" and "body" do occur in translations of Zen texts, which might suggest that they are separate things. But the use of these terms also is compatible with a view that has been held by some Western philosophers: that "the mind" refers to an amalgam of the body's consciousness along with various stylistic features of the body and features reflecting intention or motivation. Thoughts, emotions, and insights, in short, would be viewed as activities of a body or bodies. This is a plausible interpretation of the Zen view, especially because of remarks that enlightenment should be evident in the body of the enlightened person.

In no. 26 of The Gateless Gate, for example, a Zen teacher watches two monks rolling up a bamboo screen and—apparently simply on the basis of this observation—remarks that the (spiritual) state of the first is better than that of the second. Eugen Herrigel, in *Zen in the Art of Archery*, reports that he had been counseled to learn Zen in Japan in the context of a specific skilled activity, archery. When he was ready to return to his native Germany, his Zen teacher asked him to send photos of himself drawing the bow, so that the teacher could see if he was maintaining the spiritual discipline.

Presumably if a spiritual advance is evident in the body, this should be even more true of enlightenment. This claim might seem to conflict with Zen remarks quoted earlier, such as "The beauty of my garden is invisible." However, the point of such remarks is *not* that there is some hidden psychic realm that is the entire home of enlightenment.

Rather, it is that the marks of enlightenment are subtle, and the vast majority of people will be unable to spot them.

One of the features of Zen enlightenment, as we have seen, is heightened awareness of the detail and texture of the world. The average person will take in the broad outline of a fact: there is a woman or man doing such and such. Someone with successful Zen training, though, can pick up on a lot more than this, including psychological and spiritual qualities of someone encountered.

The Platform Sutra

The Platform Sutra is a foundational text of the variety of Zen Buddhism, the Rinzai (sudden enlightenment) school, that is best known in the West. It purports to be the work of the legendary sixth patriarch, Hui-neng, who is thought to have lived in China from 638 to 713 CE; although scholars think that the actual date of the work may be later. The Platform Sutra includes a narrative of Hui-neng's life and also contains philosophical observations that are shaped to provide guidance for someone interested in Zen.

The legend of Hui-neng centers on a dramatic contest to be the successor to the dying fifth patriarch. The odds-on favorite was the head monk of the monastery, Shen-hsiu. His philosophy was put forward in a verse that (in the Philip Yampolsky translation of the Platform Sutra, p. 130) reads as follows:

> The body is like the Bodhi tree,
> The mind is like a clear mirror.
> At all times we must strive to polish it,
> And must not let the dust collect.

Hui-neng, who was uneducated and did menial jobs in the monastery, put up a competitive verse. In the translation in D. T. Suzuki's *The Zen Philosophy of No-Mind* it reads

> There is no Bodhi-tree,
> Nor stand of mirror bright.
> Since all is void,
> Where can the dust alight?

As the legend has it, Hui-neng won the contest and became the sixth patriarch.

The notion that all is void brings us back to a cluster of interrelated concepts that we looked at earlier: *mu, shunyata,* and Buddha nature. We need to remain mindful that words like "void" and "emptiness" do not denote vacuum or sheer negation of any being. Much like the "nothingness" in Jean-Paul Sartre's *Being and Nothingness,* they stand instead for openness and indeterminacy, the lack of an entirely definite nature.

Any nonspecialist commentator must be hesitant in attempting to explicate further. Let me say that there seem to be three related ideas involved in the void to which Hui-neng refers, and in the idea of no-mind that Suzuki treats as central to Zen. One is the idea of what Yampolsky (see p. 141) renders as "formlessness." This itself has two aspects: there are the arguments of Nagarjuna to the effect that nothing has a definite nature, so that flat assertions always are not really acceptable. There also are the empirical data, captured so memorably in the Zhuangzi, of the fluidity of self. Perhaps all of reality is formless, but this is, as it were, overdetermined in the case of the human self.

Second, there is the traditional Buddhist claim, at the root of the doctrine of *anatman,* that there is nothing like a mind-substance. Recall the opening verse of the Dhammapada, that all we are is made up of our thoughts. It is tempting to think of the mind as, if not a substance, then at least a place where thoughts and emotions occur. But the traditional Buddhist view is that this is superstition or philosophically lazy thinking. The reality is that there are just the thoughts and emotions. There is no mind (above and beyond these), and in this sense too there is a void.

We are left with the flow of thoughts and emotions. There is nothing inherently wrong with these, which may be the explanation of Hui-neng's claim (Yampolsky, p. 135) that enlightenment and intuitive wisdom are there from the outset and merely need to be recovered. It also fits the view (see Suzuki, p. 19) that passions, provided they are understood and put in their place, are compatible with enlightenment.

What goes wrong in life is that thoughts and emotions go on, taking on a life of their own; and they (so to speak) have us instead of our having them. We cling to things and people, this being the attachment that is central to desire. The third idea that seems to me to be at work in the talk of the void and of no-mind is that of a cessation of thought, allowing us, as it were, to unhook from the world. Meditative practice (p. 138) can aim at this.

D. T. Suzuki points out the crucial importance in the process of Zen enlightenment of knowing what is self-nature. This can be no ordinary kind of knowledge. As we have seen, mind and self are formless and are emptiness (*shunyata*). What we normally would like to think of as knowledge is "relative" and concerned with dualities, in that it features a split between a subject (the knower) and an object (the known). We cannot have anything like this "knowledge" of *shunyata*. But *shunyata* is constantly with us. We can (p. 60) be in touch with it by means of a nongrasping, nondiscrimination.

Conclusion

The chief characteristics of Zen that will have emerged are the fluid ease and the improvisatory nature of the behavior and thought that it recommends, along with a determined lack of seriousness. Seriousness is symptomatic of the philosophical errors that center on the idea of literal truth and absolute categories. It also is a stumbling block to anyone who would like to attain emotional freedom and natural ease in the world.

In the light of all this, anyone who attempts to express the thought of Zen in terms of formal arguments strongly risks being ludicrous. Nevertheless, this is a book for (among others) philosophy students and philosophers. Clearly, there is a great deal of philosophy at work in Zen, and one way of bringing this out is in terms of patterns of (implicit) argument.

So here goes. Let me say that *something like* the three arguments that follow is implicit in the philosophical core of Zen. There certainly is no *precise* pattern of argument, and for that matter the arguments function mainly as starting points for something different: the moral psychology of liberation.

1. Most people would like to arrive at a literal and definitively correct rendering of the realities in their lives. But (a) the arguments provided by Nagarjuna show that any literal claims about reality lead to contradiction. Also (b) implicit in the Zhuangzi is the argument that any reality can be viewed from an unlimited number of perspectives. Hence it always is possible that some perspective not yet entertained will be superior to those now available to us. From (a) and (b) it follows that we cannot attribute any definitive, objective form to any reality.

   Hence any reality is formless. This is true of our own reality: that is, what we are. The arguments show not only this, but also that there is no final knowledge or literal truth. What we are, and also what we encounter, is a kind of nothingness: a void in the sense of having no formulatable or objective form.

2. Experience shows that the void that is the self is highly fluid. People change, and indeed sometimes have conversion experiences. Their spiritual tendencies can respond to training. Anyone is capable of progress. It follows from this body of experience that anyone has a Buddha nature, if by a Buddha nature is meant a formless nature that has spiritual potential.

3. There is a great temptation to regard this Buddha nature as either equivalent to a mind, or as being located in a mind. But there are arguments going back to Buddha's original teaching, that we should not posit the reality of what does not figure in experience. Introspection reveals to us a swirl of thoughts, feelings, urges, and the like. It does not reveal anything psychic that is stable and invariant, nor does it reveal a mind-substance in which (or as which) the swirl can be located.

Hence there is no mind.

It should be said hastily that this is not intended as a literal truth. Treating it as if it were one would be itself both foolish and dangerous. Rather, the claim that there is no mind should be taken as rejecting the unthinking assumption that there is a special psychic substance or location at work in our lives. It is a denial of this assumption, but not in the manner of anything like a flat contradiction that posits a definite reality opposite to what it denies. Rather, it is a way of insisting that the assumption is highly misleading, and that we should attempt to think in a clearer and more sophisticated way.

Of course you have a mind *if* by that is meant that you have thoughts, feelings, urges, and the like. The trouble is that there is a persistent, natural wrongheadedness that makes virtually all of us read more into the claim that we have minds. Once we can get to see the thoughts, feelings, and urges as free-floating, we will be better able not to take them seriously. This will help us to avoid being attached to their objects, or being fixated on patterns of thought or of life. We really are formless and fluid in our natures. The trick is to live as if we are comfortable with that.

It should be said again that these arguments—to the extent to which they capture underlying elements of Zen thought—merely are starting points in a way of living. The subtleties of what it is like to be liberated can hardly be captured in any formalistic way. Instead, one needs a series of portraits and anecdotes, which is what *Zen Flesh, Zen Bones* provides.

Recommended Reading

A good general account of Zen is Thomas P. Kasulis, *Zen Action, Zen Person* (Honolulu: University Press of Hawaii, 1981).

A very usable translation of the Platform Sutra, along with a good deal of scholarly background, is provided by Philip Yampolsky *(The Platform Sutra of the Sixth Patriarch*: New York, Columbia University Press, 1967).

D. T. Suzuki's *The Zen Doctrine of No-Mind*, 2nd edition (London: Rider, 1969) contains an elegantly written and very readable account of central philosophical ideas of Zen, keyed to the thought of the sixth patriarch. Suzuki surely ranks with Joseph Conrad and Vladimir Nabokov as a stylist among those for whom English is a second language. For the anti-realist arguments of Nagarjuna, see Jay Garfield's *The Fundamental Wisdom of the Middle Way* (New York: Oxford University Press, 1995).

An interesting introduction to visual materials connected with Zen can be found in Anne Bancroft's *Zen. Direct Pointing at Reality* (London: Thames and Hudson, 1979).

Some of the texture of Zen practice is conveyed in Eshin Nishimura's *Unsui: A Diary of Zen Monastic Life,* edited by Bardwell Smith and illustrated by G. Satoh (Honolulu: University Press of Hawaii, 1973).

NINE

CLASSIC ASIAN PHILOSOPHIES AS
GUIDES TO LIFE

It should be abundantly clear that each of the eight classic texts that have been discussed is distinctive, offering something of importance (that is worth arguing about) not to be found in the other seven. Readers with a taste for generalization sometimes are tempted to suppose that there is some central element, some core of spirituality or "perennial philosophy" that most or all share. If what is looked for is deep doctrine, or a common specific emphasis, this is simply not true.

Nevertheless, there are one or two common features in the *pursuit* that these eight texts all represent, even if these features are extremely nonspecific and even if the results of the pursuits vary considerably. All of the texts attempt to present features of the human condition that many people will not have taken in. They then draw conclusions about how, in the light of these findings, we ought to live.

Someone whose exposure to Asian philosophy has been limited might be given the impression, especially by the selection of texts, that Asian philosophy is oriented toward problems of life in a way that is often not paralleled in Western philosophy. There is some truth to this. There certainly are classic Indian and Chinese texts that center on abstract issues, such as those in formal logic, that have little immediate connection with problems of life. But these simply lack the fame and the influence of the texts I have discussed. There are no Asian counterparts to Western figures such as Descartes, Leibniz, and Bishop Berkeley, famous major philosophers whose best-known philosophical results had only a rather slight immediate relation to problems of life. The eight texts we have considered are, I think, the most famous and influential ones in their cultures. They all make clear that their findings about the human condition are intended to have a major immediate relation to the direction of our lives.

It should be emphasized that this generalization is very broad and nonspecific indeed. Some of the eight texts (The Upanishads, for example) center on findings that are primarily metaphysical, enabling us to view the entire universe (and our place in it) in a new way. At the other extreme, the findings about the human condition presented by Confucius and Mencius have no tincture of metaphysics. They concern instead human moral psychology and its political ramifications.

The conclusions about how we ought to live also are extremely diverse. It has been suggested (by Victor Mair in the introduction to his translation of the Daodejing (Tao Te Ching), and more recently by Herbert Fingarette) that there are strong similarities between that work and the Bhagavad Gita, which might suggest similarities between those who live in the light of the Daodejing and those who live in the light of the Bhagavad Gita. Even if there is something to this, the similarities are much less between those who (in the period before the Bhagavad Gita was written) attempted to live in the light of the Upanishads and those whose primary influence was the Daodejing or (to push the traditions apart even further) the Zhuangzi. Further away still is the guidance about life to be found in Confucius and Mencius. Nor should we assume that a life according to Mencius, who periodically emphasizes a voluntary effort to activate a normally present element of human nature, is absolutely identical with the one that Confucius recommends. And no one also should be tempted to identify the direction of life prompted by Buddha (who, as the German philosopher Friedrich Nietzsche said, fell under "the spell and illusion of morality") with that to be found in the great Daoist texts, or to conflate Buddhist detachment with Confucian engagement.

Thus we have been presented with eight recommended ways of life—and perhaps with more than eight, if we bear in mind that some of the texts (e.g., the Bhagavad Gita) present options, while others (both Buddhist and Confucian) appear willing to tailor recommendations to people's spiritual or moral potentials. In this final chapter we can examine how the texts provide guidance in life. This will require two related lines of inquiry. We need to look closely at what is recommended: that is, what are intended to be the ethical or practical results of philosophy. But we need also to examine how the findings about the human condition that each text supplies support the recommendations about life that ensue.

Correcting Mistakes in One's Life

The ethical results of the texts best can be compared if we begin with two generalizations to which, in very broad outline but not in similar detail, their authors all would subscribe. One is that normal human nature, as manifested in the very early part of life, is not entirely adequate, and indeed may have traps or hazards built into it. The second is that some of us, when we are past the very early part of life, are capable of reconsidering who and what we are, and can arrive at a much improved second nature.

The Indian texts, both Hindu and Buddhist, hold the first thesis in an especially dramatic form. The human nature of the vast majority of people is built around an illusion. The illusion is that of a real, discrete individual self.

In the Hindu formulations, this is not a total mistake: it is an illusion, not a delusion. The deeper reality, though, is that each of us is at the core an *atman* that is identical to Brahman. Our sense of individuality is a superficial take on the world, and in this way a mistake. In early Buddhist philosophy the sense of individuality is based on the mistaken assumption that one has an *atman*. Once you realize that there is no *atman* within you, you can see more clearly that the boundaries between you and others are artificial, subject to happenstance, and largely meaningless.

What has just been characterized is a kind of metaphysical mistake that all of us, from the points of view of Hinduism and those of Buddhism, are prone to. We are programmed to get it wrong, they think. The mistake might seem to be one merely of abstract philosophy. But it has motivational consequences.

Both traditions insist that, because of our mistaken sense of individual self, we become ensnared in a network of desires that, whether they lead to pleasure or frustration, inevitably contribute to an addictive pattern of further desire. The addiction is disturbing, destroying peace of mind and any possibility of spiritual concentration. The Buddhist texts especially insist that the bottom line of a life of desire is suffering. This will be the case throughout life in general, but becomes especially prominent in sickness and old age, and when we are facing death. Suffering is the human condition, Buddha says, . . . unless we follow his way out.

In short, both Hindu and early Buddhist texts hold that "normal" human nature is sick. To avoid a tense and meaningless life, we need to replace this initial nature with something else. Given the ways in which normal human nature is entrenched, especially by the time we are old enough to reconsider it, this is a monumental task, requiring much effort and concentration. We need to change our nature and to struggle against the way we have been programmed.

The Chinese texts by and large (to continue generalizing broadly) do not have quite so bleak a view of normal human nature. They all do hold that it needs to be shaped, adapted, or modified. None believes that the life of the average person can be considered very good to have, even if the person whose life it is remains satisfied.

It might seem at first that Mencius is an exception to the generalization about the defects of normal human nature. He, after all, holds that benevolent urges, the source of goodness, are inherent. In that sense he is clearly an optimist about human nature.

Nevertheless, any close reading of Mencius makes it clear that there was a huge gulf, in his view, between having benevolent urges (which any normal person sometimes has) and being a good person. Mencius may waver in his assessment of how to bridge this gulf. He sometimes suggests that an effort of will can make a difference. But on the whole we can take for granted his support of the original Confucian program of gradual self-cultivation by means of the classics, ritual, and music.

It also is clear that Mencius thinks that a very desirable life requires this self-cultivation. The standard Confucian view (which Mencius shares) is that only someone who has achieved the right kind of refinement can gain inner satisfactions that render him or her less concerned than the average person is about luck and the vicissitudes of life. Further, when Mencius speaks of his high energy level, made possible by elimination of psychic conflicts and cross-purposes, there is a strong suggestion that the average person lacks this. The average person in his view also lacks, whatever his or her urges are, reliable and consistent benevolence in behavior.

It goes without saying that Confucius, also, thinks that original nature needs to be shaped by a sustained program of cultivation in order to be worth something. There is a clear elitism in this. Confucius shows no sign of thinking that most people would respond very well to such a program. It is suitable for those of greater capacities.

The Daoist texts, on the face of it, have more interest in, and respect for, early human nature. Perhaps there is an image of human nature—before it has been corrupted by concepts and norms—that is parallel to the Daodejing's vision of a primitive integrated society from which we have declined? Both the Daodejing and the Zhuangzi at some points suggest that a very simple person may be less far from the style of life characteristic of enlightenment than clever people generally are.

Nevertheless, simplicity (unless it amounts to idiocy) is no protection against the corruption (corruption, that is, from the Daoist point of view) that involves having desires and worrying about the future. We are given far less of a picture of how someone becomes a good Daoist than we are of how someone becomes, say, a good Zen Buddhist. But it is clear that, whatever the program of self-shaping is, it amounts to an inoculation against the pathology of attachment and desire.

This is of course true also of Zen Buddhist training. The life of the accomplished Zen Buddhist or Daoist may have some features of placidity and fluidity of behavior that resemble aspects of the lives of idiots and near-idiots. But the underlying sophistication does differ sharply. And the Zen Buddhist or Daoist has seen through many psychological dangers to which the near-idiot is not immune.

Thus—to varying degrees and in varying ways—all of the texts discussed in this book agree that the best kind of life requires something better than normal human nature. This is not a point that would normally occur to a small child, nor would the child be in much of a position to do something about it. There is a period in many lives—usually in the late teenage years or in someone's twenties—when two things come together. First, a young woman or man achieves enough independence of mind to be able to judge the tendencies of her or his life thus far, and to reconsider their value. Secondly, there will be enough autonomy in the management of life so that, if drastic revision seems called for, the young woman or man can try to do something about it.

People in this position will be important members of the target audience of all of the texts. There is of course no reason why someone who is older could not take to heart something in one of these texts and attempt to act on it. What the texts all say is "Here are some reasons (having to do with the human condition) that you might change your life. Here are ways in which it could be better."

The great Hindu texts thus in effect urge a retreat from the world—which in the earlier period often was a literal retreat, but after the Bhagavad Gita could be a psychological retreat of greater detachment—so that one can work through the implications of oneness with the universe. The Dhammapada urges the spiritually ambitious members of its audience to foresake ordinary life in the world, and to become a nun or a monk, concentrating on the elimination of sense of self and of desires. *Zen Flesh, Zen Bones* much later offers examples of people who have done this, influenced especially by the later idea of *shunyata* (nothingness/complete openness). The Confucian texts in effect encourage young men to devote themselves to an education of refinement, like the young men who left their ordinary lives in order to live and travel with Confucius. (It also of course speaks to the ideals of those who are older and have cultivated themselves to some extent, but always could go further.) The Daoist texts offer visions of naturalness and emotional freedom that might well incite hearers or readers to work on themselves in this direction.

In all of these cases, what is presented as an ideal, a goal, or a range of desirable possibilities is a life as a better kind of person. Self-transformation is what is urged. In no case will it be quick or easy. Even the Rinzai school of Zen Buddhism, which highlights sudden enlightenment, makes it abundantly clear that long and strenuous training is required before the final breakthrough is possible.

Whether self-transformation is possible depends in part on the stubbornness of original nature and instincts. Two psychologists, Keller and Marian Breland, tell an instructive story about a raccoon used in an experiment on learning. Tasks were set for the raccoon, a very smart animal; and it was rewarded for successful completion with a coin, which it then could use to get food. The raccoon did well at this sequence. The experimenters decided to make the learning tasks more complicated and difficult, requiring the raccoon to earn two coins, and then use the two coins to get food. At this point the experiment broke down. Raccoons prefer cleanliness, cleaning items of food by rubbing them against other items. This food-related instinct, so useful in dealing with, say, crayfish, ruined the experiment. Given the two food-related coins, the raccoon simply kept rubbing them together.

Perhaps this failure followed from the nature of raccoons. The Brelands give other examples of animals for whom learned behavior, in their view, drifts toward instinctive behavior. What about humans? Hindu and Buddhist philosophers especially would say that dismal features of life, including suffering and also a shortage of joy, follow from our natures and instincts. But their claim is that we, unlike the raccoon that ruined the experiment, can (with considerable work) eliminate the unfortunate features of our nature and arrive at something much better.

The Confucian and Daoist criticisms of normal human nature, as I have indicated, are less radical than those to be found in classic Indian texts. But Confucians and Daoists too would have us go beyond the natures with which we began (and which the average person more or less retains). Self-fashioning is a central theme of these philosophies also.

What we are urged to arrive at might be termed a second nature. Certain things that are natural for the average person will no longer be natural for us, and we will have come to find some different ways of thinking and behaving natural. Some of the texts, notably the Upanishads and the Dhammapada, probably should be read as positing an ideal state that a human being can reach, after which she or he remains the same. I think that the Daoist and Confucian texts are best read as pointing instead toward continued possibilities of further development or refinement. But, be that as it may, all of the texts discussed can be seen as pointing toward the hope of becoming a different kind of person: not merely in terms of occasional occurrences of different kinds of thought and behavior, but different in one's nature and the ongoing moment-to-moment character of life.

There remains the question of how the two elements that I have claimed to find in all of these texts are related to each other. How, that is, are the claims about the human condition related to the ethical claims about how we best should live? Is there any relation at all? And if there is, is it one of logic?

The "Is" and the "Ought"

The relation between claims about the human condition and the guidance in life to which these give rise can be related to a long Western tradition of wondering whether ethical judgments can be logically derived from facts. The facts that might be starting points have sometimes been presented as biological, or as facts about human psychology, or as metaphysical. The issue often is referred to as that of whether we can get the "ought" from the "is."

David Hume famously contended that we cannot derive the "ought" from the "is," a position seemingly amplified in G. E. Moore's 1903 book *Principia Ethica*. Moore assailed what he called the "naturalistic fallacy," but also devoted a chapter to attacking attempts to derive ethical judgments from metaphysical claims. Both of these treatments of the issue, though, raise more complicated questions than at first may seem the case. If Moore was right, then on what basis can anyone arrive at ethical judgments? Moore's answer ("intuition") is discouragingly unspecific, and the obvious alternative (which then was endorsed by A. J. Ayer and others) was to regard ethical judgments as arbitrary expressions of feeling or attitude that are incapable of being true or false. In Hume's case, a major complication is deciding what he really meant. Some commentators have suggested that Hume, in his stricture on deriving the "ought" from the "is," merely intended to block certain kinds of deductive inferences. He appears to accept an ethics that, in his own account, derives its justification from facts about human nature.

Someone coming for the first time upon this long-standing debate about the "is" and the "ought" might well feel divided. On one hand, many philosophers have made the plausible point that whether facts get us to an ethical conclusion depends very much on how we react to the facts. We are not logically compelled to react in one way rather than another.

But the obvious further step—dismissively regarding ethical judgments as merely expressive of personal attitudes and tastes—may seem implausible in the light of cases in which people have the sense of having *learned* to see the wrongness or the desirability of something. There is no obvious absurdity in someone's claim to have arrived through experience at a better ethical view than she or he previously had had. It seems plausible to regard some attitudes as more "apt" (to borrow language from a recent writer, Allan Gibbard) than others.

But if this is the case, then ethical judgments that express apt attitudes will be more justified than ones that express inappropriate ones. How do we support a claim that one ethical judgment is more justified than another? How can we get to such a conclusion *except* from facts? What else do we have to go on?

This large and difficult issue, like many central questions of philosophy, can look very different to people who have different starting points. Formulations of just what the issue is are in themselves controversial. We also need not assume that there are only two possible answers: that is, that ethical judgments either simply are logically derivable from facts or simply are not.

What we are willing to consider as logic, or as a logical relation, is one of the relevant factors. A highly traditional view in the West is that there are two forms of logic: deductive (the kind of reasoning exemplified in mathematics and in traditional formal logic, in which one can infer a conclusion that would have to be true given certain starting points), and inductive (the kind of reasoning that infers a likelihood that cases not yet experienced of something will fit the pattern of cases that have been experienced). It seems highly implausible that the relation between facts and ethical conclusions fits either of these patterns. But if, in the light of certain facts, an ethical conclusion emerges as more reasonable—as having a stronger case for it than would have been true absent those facts—why can we not regard this as a sort of logical relation that is neither deductive nor inductive?

Two late twentieth-century books, Thomas Nagel's *The Possibility of Altruism* (1970) and Derek Parfit's *Reasons and Persons* (1984), argue for claims in the metaphysics of self (that is, claims about what one's personal identity and relation to other people amount to) that the authors contend "ground" or "support" ethical positions. In neither book is a formal logic of grounding or supporting outlined. But, again, we are left with the thought that there is some kind of relation between facts about the human condition, on one hand, and ethical conclusions, on the other. This is a thought that I have argued is central to all of the texts discussed in this book.

Any book about philosophy at some point should lead to a sense of what it is like to "do" philosophy (that is, to think independently about it). Typically this is a rich and stressful experience. Often part of it is a sense of having the ground move beneath one's feet, as the ideas and meanings you rely on turn out not to be necessarily fixed.

Suppose we continue to take the issue as "How can facts about the human condition be related to ethical conclusions?" What then are facts? There is an unthinking tendency to imagine facts as like bits of reality that we almost might bump into. But anti-realists will insist that any "fact" includes an element of "seeing as," thus playing a part in an interpretative take on the world. Ethical judgments also, notoriously, involve an interpretative take on the world, at least insofar as we normally would expect two people with different ethical views to have different pictures of what the world is like.

There must be a difference between ethical judgments and judgments of fact, one might think. But what is it? An obvious thought is that ethical judgments seem designed to get people to behave in certain ways, or at least they typically do. (There are cases in which someone makes an ethical judgment but does not seem to care how anyone behaves.) Judgments of fact, though, sometimes seem designed also to guide behavior. Think of "What you are about to drink is poison." Again there is the nagging thought that there surely is some difference between two kinds of judgments. But maybe it is a difference in some cases and not in all cases?

There also is the thought that, if there is a class of ethical judgments and a class of judgments of fact, there might be some overlap. Might there be ethical facts? At least one major philosopher, Elizabeth Anscombe, suggested this. She used the example of having asked her grocer to deliver potatoes, and his having delivered them. It was a "brute fact," she insisted, that she owed him money for the potatoes. This is a fact about, among other things, what she ought to do (i.e., pay him the money). If it is a fact, then surely it is an ethical fact.

Whether or not there are ethical facts, we are left with the question of how claims about what the world is like or about human moral psychology can be related to ethical claims that we might well hesitate to connect with "ethical facts." Take, for example, Buddha's claim that we would have a better life if we eliminated our sense of individual self and all of our desires. Even someone who accepted Buddha's claim might well regard what it talks about as a less plausible candidate for "ethical fact" status than Anscombe's owing money to her grocer. But, conversely, even someone who does not accept Buddha's claim might agree that there is a stronger case for it if we accept what Buddha says about the causes of suffering than if we do not. So—we again might ask—just what is the relation between Buddha's moral psychology and his ethical conclusion?

It may be that questions of this sort will continue to baffle us until we recognize that there are more kinds of reasoning—or of appropriate reason giving—than we normally recognize. There have been similar difficulties in understanding the forms of explanation common in various disciplines. It might seem tempting to insist on a single model, say the one in which an explanation works by pointing out that what is at hand is an instance of a recognized valid covering law. This is neat, but it looks as if it distorts what practitioners of various disciplines often are doing when they offer explanations. One philosopher of history, W. B. Gallie, suggested that a good deal of historical explanation consisted of a "thickening" of narrative so that what was to be explained no longer would look surprising.

In somewhat this way, it may be that each of our eight texts can be viewed as "thickening" its narrative of the human condition, so that certain kinds of guidance in life seem a natural continuation of the picture of the world that is provided. Should this be viewed as logic, or as coherent storytelling? Any reader can explore her or his own view on this.

What remains true, whatever one thinks about the relation between facts and values, is that a philosophy can combine—with the
appearance of seamlessness—a picture of what the world is like with a
system of ethical guidance. All of the texts discussed in this book do
this. Any one of them, if you were entirely to agree with the philosophy, would drastically change both your view of the world, and also
how you lived.

Recommended Reading

The themes related to ethical guidance are taken up in various ways in three
previous books of mine, all published by Oxford University Press. They
are *Character* (1991), *Value . . . and What Follows* (1999), and *Learning
from Asian Philosophy* (1999). The relation between claims about the
human condition, on one hand, and ethical conclusions, on the other, is
examined at length in my "Metaphysics as Prologomenon to Ethics,"
Midwest Studies in Philosophy (2000). Fact and value are examined in
"How Values Congeal Into Facts," *Ratio* (2000).

Hume's accounts of the "is"—"ought" relation (both the very short and dramatic version, and the extremely long and nuanced one) are contained in
Book 3 of *A Treatise of Human Nature.*

A brief and readable discussion of what facts are is contained in Bede Run-
dle's *Facts* (London: Duckworth, 1993).

G. E. M. Anscombe's "Modern Moral Philosophy" (*Philosophy* 33, 1958, 1–19)
includes the example of the fact of her owing money to her grocer for
potatoes.

W. B. Gallie's account of historical explanation can be found in "Explanations
in History and the Genetic Sciences," in *Theories of History,* ed. Patrick
Gardiner, 386–402 (Glencoe: Free Press, 1959).

In the chapter I compared ways in which it might be held that we can alter
our human natures with the failure of a raccoon to overcome raccoon
nature. For the raccoon, see Breland and Breland, "The Misbehavior of
Organisms," *American Psychologist* 1961, 16, 681–84.

INDEX